My eLab | Efficient teaching, effective learning

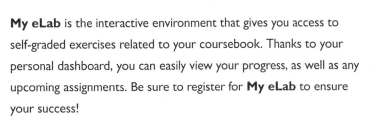

My eLab is the interactive environment that gives you access to self-graded exercises related to your coursebook. Thanks to your personal dashboard, you can easily view your progress, as well as any upcoming assignments. Be sure to register for **My eLab** to ensure your success!

TO REGISTER

❶ Go to **http://mybookshelf.pearsonerpi.com**

❷ Click on "NOT REGISTERED YET?" and follow the instructions. When asked for your access code, please type the code provided underneath the blue sticker.

❸ To access **My eLab** at any time, go to http://mybookshelf.pearsonerpi.com. **Bookmark this page for quicker access.**

Access to My eLab is valid for 12 months from the date of registration.

WARNING! This book CANNOT BE RETURNED if the access code has been uncovered.

Note: Once you have registered, you will need to join your online class. Ask your teacher to provide you with the class ID.

TEACHER Access Code

To obtain an access code for My eLab, please contact your Pearson ELT consultant.

I 800 263-3678
assistance@pearsonerpi.com

🐦 @HelpPearsonERPI

W134145 (A36728)

2457

leap

Learning English for Academic Purposes

Second Edition

READING AND WRITING

JULIA WILLIAMS

PEARSON

Montréal

Managing Editor
Patricia Hynes

Project Editor
Linda Barton

Proofreader
Mairi MacKinnon

Coordinator, Rights and Permissions
Pierre Richard Bernier

Text Rights and Permissions
Marie-Chantal Masson

Art Director
Hélène Cousineau

Graphic Design Coordinator
Lyse LeBlanc

Book and Cover Design
Frédérique Bouvier

Book Layout
Interscript

Dedication

As always, my thanks (and much more) go to Wayne, Sam and Scott Parker and to my parents, Ron and Carolyn Williams, for their support, commiseration, empathy and encouragement.

Text Credits

Chapter 1, pp. 12–14, 20–21 Excerpts from "Youth Involvement and Positive Development in Sport" by J. Côté & J. Fraser-Thomas reprinted with permission by Pearson Canada Inc.

Chapter 2, p. 26 Excerpt from "Notes for International Students" © Association of Universities and Colleges of Canada. pp. 29–31 "How Do I Choose the Right Program for Me?" by Erin Millar reprinted with permission of the author. pp. 43–46 Excerpt from "Trends in Higher Education" © Association of Universities and Colleges of Canada.

Chapter 3, p. 52 Excerpt from "Understanding Marketing Processes and Consumer Behaviour" by R. W. Griffin, R. J. Ebert, F. A. Starke & M. D. Lang reprinted with permission by Pearson Canada Inc. pp. 57–61, 66–68 Excerpts from "Understanding Consumer and Business Buyer Behaviour" by G. Armstrong, P. Kotler, V. Trifts, L. Buchwitz & P. Finlayson reprinted with permission by Pearson Canada Inc.

Chapter 4, pp. 72–73 Excerpt from "Product Strategy" by K. Tuckwell reprinted with permission by Pearson Canada Inc. pp. 77–79 Excerpt from "Brand Strategy and Management" by G. Armstrong, P. Kotler, V. Trifts, L. Buchwitz & P. Finlayson reprinted with permission by Pearson Canada Inc. pp. 86–88 Excerpt from "Sustainable Marketing, Social Responsibility and Ethics" by G. Armstrong, P. Kotler, V. Trifts, L. Buchwitz & P. Finlayson reprinted with permission by Pearson Canada Inc.

Chapter 5, pp. 94–99 Excerpts from Sutton, Amy L., ed. *Complementary and Alternative Medicine Sourcebook*, 4th ed. pp. 104–107 Excerpt from *Humanizing Modern Medicine: An Introductory Philosophy of Medicine* by J. Marcum with kind permission from Springer Science + Business Media B.V.

Chapter 6, pp. 117–119, 125–127 Excerpts from *Infection and Immunity*, 3rd ed. by J. Playfair & G. Bancroft reprinted with permission. pp. 122–123 Excerpt from *Vaccine Anxieties: Global Science, Child Health and Society* by M. Leach & J. Fairhead reprinted with permission of J. Fairhead. pp. 130–133 "Vaccine Brain Damage: Aftermath of Hepatitis B Shots" by Lucia Morgan McHardy reprinted with permission of the author.

Chapter 7, pp. 139, 148 Excerpts from *How Risky Is It, Really? Why Our Fears Don't Always Match the Facts* by D. Ropeik reprinted with permission of the author. pp. 145–147 Excerpt from *RISK: A Practical Guide for Deciding What's Really Safe and What's Really Dangerous in the World Around You* by David Ropeik and George Gray. Copyright © 2002 by David Ropeik and George Gray. Reprinted by permission of Houghton Mifflin Hartcourt Publishing Company. All rights reserved. pp. 150–152 "Vaccination" by P. J. Lachmann © The British Academy 2002.

Chapter 8, pp. 160–162 "'Slow Food' the New Happy Meal" by M. McQuigge © *The Canadian Press*. pp. 164–166 Excerpt from *In Praise of Slowness: How a Worldwide Movement Is Challenging the Cult of Speed* by Carl Honoré. Copyright © 2004 Carl Honoré. Reprinted by permission of Knopf Canada. pp. 171–174 Excerpt from *Slow Food Nation: Why Our Food Should Be Good, Clean, and Fair* by C. Petrini © Rizzoli Ex Libris.

© ÉDITIONS DU RENOUVEAU PÉDAGOGIQUE INC. (ERPI), 2012
ERPI publishes and distributes PEARSON ELT products in Canada.

1611 Crémazie Boulevard East, 10th Floor
Montréal, Québec H2M 2P2
Canada
Telephone: 1 800 263-3678
Fax: 514 334-4720
information@pearsonerpi.com
pearsonerpi.com

Registration of copyright – Bibliothèque et Archives nationales du Québec, 2012
Registration of copyright – Library and Archives Canada, 2012

Printed in Canada   6789   HLN   18 17 16 15
ISBN 978-2-7613-4145-5   134145   ABCD   OF10

INTRODUCTION

It's an honour to be asked to revise a textbook, and I have greatly appreciated the chance to revise the original *Learning English for Academic Purposes*. A textbook provides a snapshot of the author's teaching experience and philosophy at the date of publication; a revision offers the opportunity to modify the material to reflect what the author has learned in the years since.

LEAP Second Edition is inspired by the same purpose as the original: to address the gaps I observed in teaching methodology between intensive non-credit ESL programs and credit EAP courses, and between credit EAP courses and academic content courses. I found the EAP environment was necessarily focused on evaluation to generate a final grade. I felt students had to move from one assignment to the next without time to build on and reinforce their reading and writing skills.

There was also a gap between requirements for content courses and the material presented in EAP courses. In their content classes, students were often asked to read eighty-page chapters, understand complex vocabulary, respond to abstract questions, conduct research and write lengthy papers. Yet the materials the students were exposed to in EAP courses, however interesting, were short, and often simplistic. To this end, these chapters have been designed to incorporate a process-type approach to reading and writing skills development: short Warm-Up Assignments allow students to apply their learning—and receive feedback—before they attempt longer Final Assignments that are necessarily graded. Furthermore, the authentic materials are longer, and the viewpoints are deliberately divergent to simulate the complexity students will find outside the EAP classroom. Explicit strategy instruction assists students in processing the quantity of information in each chapter.

What is new in this second edition is the uncoupling of reading and writing from listening and speaking skills in two books, offering greater flexibility for programs with both discrete and integrated skills courses. Further, there is a more explicit focus on vocabulary, and Academic Word List words are highlighted for easy identification. Skills to support critical thinking and critical expression are also more emphasized. Skills central to academic integrity—referencing, paraphrasing and summarizing—have been retained in this edition as well as the final Models Chapter, which provides examples of all of the assignments students are asked to complete in this book.

ACKNOWLEDGEMENTS

The production of a new textbook (even a revision of an earlier textbook) requires the support of a great number of people. I would like to begin by warmly thanking my former colleagues at Carleton University, who set the stage for the development of the first edition of *Learning English for Academic Purposes*. My current colleagues at Renison University College at the University of Waterloo have also supported me with their comments, ideas and encouragement. I would especially like to thank Judi Jewinski (an author herself), who continues to create opportunities for those around her. My great appreciation goes to my teaching colleagues: Tanya Missere-Mihas, Stefan Rehm, Pat Skinner, Nancy Ozckowski, Christa Schuller, Maggie Heeney, Ron Champion, Elizabeth Matthews, Keely Cook, Christine Morgan, Dara Lane, Margy Wardell, Dianne Tyers, Audrey Olson, Andrea Brandt and Louann Nhan.

Thanks is also due to Dr. Ken Beatty, who enthusiastically took on the writing of *LEAP: Listening and Speaking,* and to the editing team at Pearson ERPI, who has been supportive and patient as we have worked through multiple drafts.

HIGHLIGHTS

The **overview** outlines the chapter objectives and features.

The **Gearing Up** section stimulates students' interest by tapping into their prior knowledge.

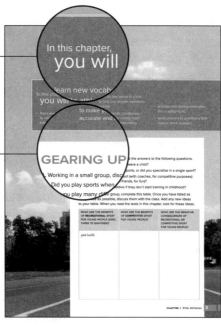

Each chapter contains three **reading** passages from a variety of predominantly Canadian sources, including academic textbooks, newspapers, magazines and Web resources. Pre- and post-reading activities and questions focus on content and meaning.

The shorter **Warm-Up Assignment** prepares students for the Final Assignment. Each chapter focuses on a different academic writing task.

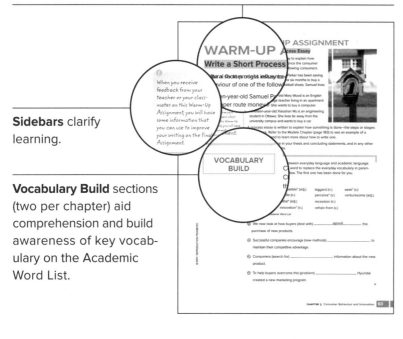

Sidebars clarify learning.

Vocabulary Build sections (two per chapter) aid comprehension and build awareness of key vocabulary on the Academic Word List.

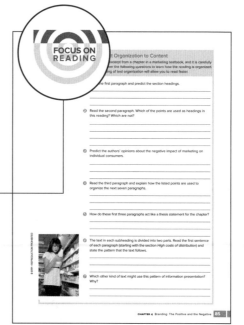

Focus on Reading develops specific skills students need to fully understand the content and structure of academic texts.

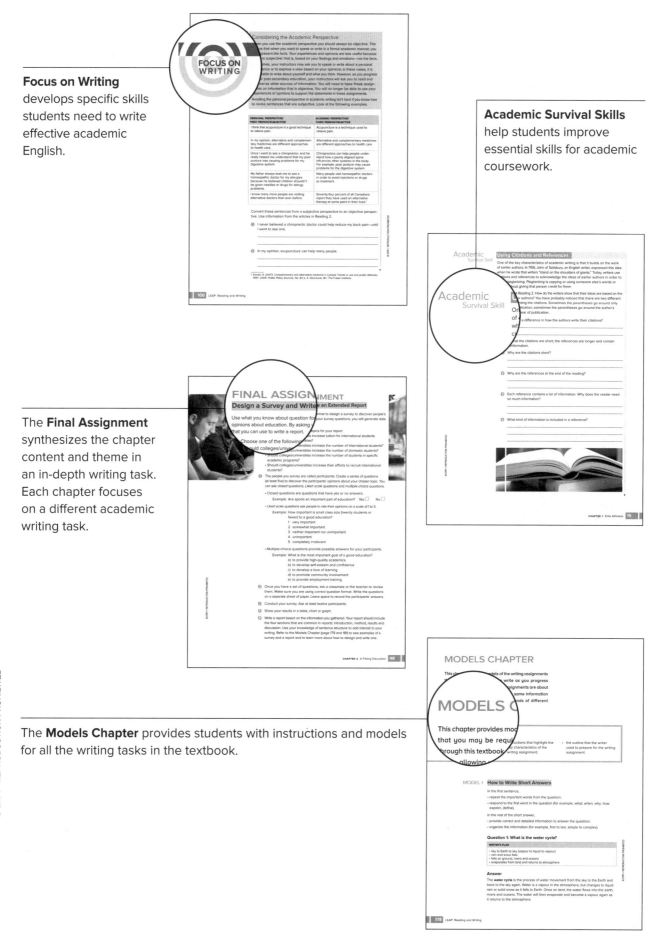

Focus on Writing
develops specific skills
students need to write
effective academic
English.

Academic Survival Skills
help students improve
essential skills for academic
coursework.

The **Final Assignment**
synthesizes the chapter
content and theme in
an in-depth writing task.
Each chapter focuses
on a different academic
writing task.

The **Models Chapter** provides students with instructions and models
for all the writing tasks in the textbook.

SCOPE AND SEQUENCE

CHAPTER	READING	WRITING
CHAPTER 1 **ELITE ATHLETES** SUBJECT AREAS: physical education, psychology	• Identifying key words in questions • Scanning for key words in texts • Using citations and references • Answering questions about reading content	• Improving your writing using specific vocabulary • Introducing examples into a text
CHAPTER 2 **A FITTING EDUCATION** SUBJECT AREA: education	• Skimming to gather information about a text • Considering the characteristics of various text types • Answering questions about reading content	• Asking questions using correct word order • Using varied sentence structure
CHAPTER 3 **CONSUMER BEHAVIOUR AND INNOVATION** SUBJECT AREAS: business, marketing	• Learning and applying "read smart" skills: identifying text organization, activating prior knowledge, predicting, taking margin notes, applying critical thinking to content • Answering questions about reading content	• Writing a thesis statement in parallel structure • Writing definitions
CHAPTER 4 **BRANDING: THE POSITIVE AND THE NEGATIVE** SUBJECT AREA: marketing	• Applying "read smart" skills • Learning independently to improve reading skills • Relating text organization to content • Answering questions about reading content	• Learning collocations to increase fluency • Learning independently to improve writing skills
CHAPTER 5 **PHILOSOPHIES OF MEDICINE** SUBJECT AREAS: medicine, philosophy	• Recognizing organizational patterns in a compare and contrast text • Answering questions about reading content	• Writing in the third person to demonstrate an objective viewpoint • Avoiding plagiarism by referencing
CHAPTER 6 **VACCINES** SUBJECT AREAS: medicine, biology	• Evaluating information • Answering questions about reading content	• Avoiding plagiarism by paraphrasing • Avoiding common errors when writing in the third person
CHAPTER 7 **RISK PERCEPTION** SUBJECT AREAS: psychology, sociology, medicine	• Skimming a text for main sections • Identifying and using expressions of cause and effect • Answering questions about reading content	• Writing conditional sentences • Avoiding plagiarism by summarizing
CHAPTER 8 **THE SLOW FOOD MOVEMENT** SUBJECT AREAS: agricultural science, health and nutrition	• Reading multi-clause, multi-phrase sentences • Answering questions about reading content	• Selecting vocabulary to express opinions • Expressing divergent opinions

WARM-UP ASSIGNMENT	FINAL ASSIGNMENT	CRITICAL THINKING
• Writing short-answer questions (2 questions)	• Taking a short-answer test (4 questions to complete in 1 hour)	• Applying vocabulary strategies: context clues, root words, prefixes and suffixes
• Writing a short report based on information gathered from class-mates (1.5 pages)	• Writing an extended report based on information gathered from a survey (minimum 5 questions, 12 participants, 2 pages)	• Designing a survey to gather data for a report
• Writing a short process essay (5-paragraph essay)	• Writing a longer process essay (2–3 pages)	• Assessing how text organization reflects communicative purpose • Evaluating the importance of content to help remember information • Applying reading concepts to write process essays
• Writing a short persuasive essay (5-paragraph essay)	• Writing a longer persuasive essay (2–3 pages)	• Using awareness of text organization to read more efficiently • Applying reading concepts to write persuasive essays
• Writing a short compare and contrast essay (1.5 pages)	• Writing a longer compare and contrast essay (2–3 pages)	• Comparing and contrasting forms of complementary and alternative medicine • Connecting philosophy to medical practice • Dividing a text into sections based on content organization
• Paraphrasing a paragraph	• Writing a process essay including the paraphrase of the Warm-Up Assignment (2–3 pages)	• Evaluating information for reliable content
• Writing a short summary (original text: 2 paragraphs)	• Writing a summary (original text: 5 paragraphs)	• Selecting expressions to reflect the strength of the relationship between cause and effect
• Writing a short persuasive essay (2 pages)	• Writing an extended persuasive essay (3–4 pages)	• Expressing divergent opinions in academic writing

TABLE OF CONTENTS

CHAPTER 1

Elite Athletes

Most people play sports recreationally—for fun and non-competitively—and enjoy the benefits of physical activity. And while competitive sport can be just as fun, elite athletes may face negative consequences due to overtraining. Is it best to play a variety of sports non-competitively, or is it worth the time and financial investment to play competitively at the highest levels and risk injury?

you will

- learn new vocabulary related to elite athletes and how they train;

- scan for key words in a text to help you answer questions quickly;

- select specific vocabulary to make your writing more accurate and interesting;

- practise introducing examples into a written text;

- write answers to questions that require short answers.

GEARING UP

A. Working in a small group, discuss the answers to the following questions.

- Did you play sports when you were a child?
- Did you play many different sports, or did you specialize in a single sport?
- Did you play competitive sport (with coaches, for competitive purposes) or recreational sport (with friends, for fun)?
- Can athletes be competitive if they don't start training in childhood?

B. Still working in your group, complete this table. Once you have listed as many ideas as possible, discuss them with the class. Add any new ideas to your table. When you read the texts in this chapter, look for these ideas.

WHAT ARE THE BENEFITS OF **RECREATIONAL** SPORT FOR YOUNG PEOPLE (AGES THREE TO EIGHTEEN)?	WHAT ARE THE BENEFITS OF **COMPETITIVE** SPORT FOR YOUNG PEOPLE?	WHAT ARE THE NEGATIVE CONSEQUENCES OF RECREATIONAL OR COMPETITIVE SPORT FOR YOUNG PEOPLE?
good health		

Three Athletes

A. Read the profiles of three athletes who have each had a different sport experience in their youth. While you read, complete the table with *yes* or *no* answers to show the differences between the athletes.

	PLAYED **MANY** SPORTS WHEN YOUNG	SPECIALIZED IN **ONE** SPORT WHEN YOUNG	INJURED BY TRAINING OR COMPETING	CONTINUED IN SPORT AS AN ADULT
Simon Whitfield Triathlon	yes			
Mary Lou Retton Gymnastics				
Scott Bradshaw Tennis				

B. When you have finished, check your answers with a partner.

C. Discuss with the class which athlete you would prefer to be. Give reasons why.

Profile One: Simon Whitfield, Triathlon

Simon Whitfield is a Canadian who won a gold medal in the 2000 Olympic Summer Games in Sydney and a silver medal in the 2008 Olympic Summer Games in Beijing. When he was young, he participated in many sports, including soccer and rowing.
5 He discovered triathlons at the age of eleven when he competed in a local Kids of Steel race. He raced on an old bike and remembers enjoying the food at the post-race barbecue. He didn't specialize in the triathlon until he was fifteen when his training intensity increased. He trained in British Columbia and Australia before competing in the Olympics. These days, he travels the country, visiting schools and encouraging
10 and inspiring children and adults. He believes that the most important element of any youth-sport program should be fun.[1]

Profile Two: Mary Lou Retton, Gymnastics

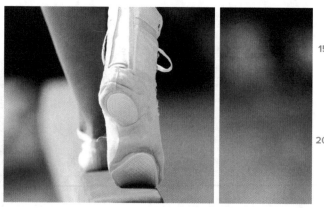

Mary Lou Retton is an American who won gold in the 1984 Olympic Games in Los Angeles when she was
15 fifteen years old. She began gymnastics training at the age of five. She trained for hours each day and competed regularly in gymnastic events. When she was fourteen, her parents supported her move to a different city so she could train with a famous coach. Her
20 training took so much time that she had to take correspondence courses to continue her education. In 1983, she hurt her wrist while training. In 1984, six weeks before the Olympics, she hurt her knee and had surgery. With exceptional determination, she recovered
25 from surgery to compete in the Games. She won gold in the all-around competition as well as a gold medal in the vault and medals in the team competition, floor exercise and uneven bars. She stopped competing after the 1984 Olympics. Today, she is a popular motivational speaker. She has had both hips replaced through surgery and suffers from arthritis due to her early gymnastics training.

1. Based on Côté, J., & Fraser-Thomas, J., (2011). Youth involvement and positive development in sport. In
   P. Crocker (Ed.), *Sport and exercise psychology: A Canadian perspective* (2nd ed., p. 247). Toronto, ON: Pearson.

30 Profile Three: Scott Bradshaw, Tennis

Between the ages of six and thirteen, Scott played hockey during the winters, and soccer and baseball in the summers. He also enjoyed tennis. His teams never won, but he almost always enjoyed playing with friends in his neighbourhood or with other teams. His parents were supportive, enrolling him in activities when he was interested,
35 letting him play soccer and baseball in their backyard and tennis at the courts in the park. He made many friends while playing sports, and he learned about winning and losing and about cooperation, responsibility, respect and self-control. As an adult, he is a teacher, coaches several school teams and plays recreational tennis.

FOCUS ON READING

Understanding Vocabulary in Context

Learning as many new words in English as you can will help you understand what you read. However, you may still see words in a reading that you are not familiar with. What do you do then?

A. Discuss with the class what you do when you see a word that you don't know. Decide as a class which ideas will help you learn and remember new words most effectively.

Here are some strategies that might help you with unfamiliar vocabulary.

Strategy 1: Guess the meaning from the context.

One of the strategies successful students use when they come across new vocabulary is to try to guess the meaning of the word from the context (or the words around the unfamiliar word).

Example: Many young athletes dream of reaching the **podium** at the Olympics.

You may not know the word *podium*, but you do know some information that will help you guess the meaning of the word. You know that

- the reading is about young athletes and how they train for sports;
- the verb in the sentence is *dream* (What do most talented athletes dream of?);
- the word *Olympics* shows you the athletes are dreaming about being successful at an international level of competition;
- "the" comes before *podium*; therefore, you know that *podium* is a noun.

You may still not understand what *podium* means, but you have a good idea what the sentence means. Now read the sentence that follows.

Example: Many young athletes dream of reaching the **podium** at the Olympics. They hope they will one day climb the **podium** to receive a medal in their sports.

The second sentence gives you more information about the meaning of the word *podium*. You now know that

- the *podium* is something that you climb onto;
- you receive medals on the *podium*.

You can probably guess that *podium* refers to the platform that winning athletes climb onto to receive their medals. Now you know the meaning of the word, and you didn't have to look it up in the dictionary.

Strategy 2: Guess the meaning from root words, prefixes and suffixes.

You can also use what you know about root words, prefixes and suffixes to help you guess the meanings of words.

> Example: The big challenge is ensuring that the young competitive athlete achieves **equilibrium** between deliberate play and deliberate practice activities.

You may not know what the word *equilibrium* means. However, you can figure out that the word is

- based on the root word *equal*, which you probably know means "the same";
- a noun, because it is the object of the verb *achieves*;
- followed by the preposition *between*, which indicates a position in the middle of two options or things.

You may also understand that the two things that follow the words *equilibrium between* (deliberate play and deliberate practice) are important parts of an athlete's training that need to be balanced. As a result, you can probably guess that the word *equilibrium* means "balance"—and you didn't need to consult a dictionary.

Remember that *prefixes* change the meaning of a word. For example:

- *pre*requisite, *pre*condition, *pre*determined (*pre-* means "before")
- *re*place, *re*think, *re*store (*re-* means "again")
- *in*considerate, *in*consistent, *in*convenient (*in-* means "not")

Suffixes change the type of word (or part of speech), but the meaning remains similar to the meaning of the root word. For example:

- activ*ity* (noun), to act (verb), active (adjective), activ*ely* (adverb)
- impres*sion* (noun), to impress (verb), impress*ive* (adjective), impress*ively* (adverb)
- rebell*ion* (noun), to rebel (verb), rebell*ious* (adjective), rebell*iously* (adverb)

Strategy 3: Keep reading without knowing the meaning of every word.

Successful students know they may have to keep reading—even if they don't know the meaning of every word—in order to finish the reading quickly. Sometimes it isn't necessary to know the meaning of every word to understand the meaning of the reading.

> Example: Athletes involved in deliberate practice activities may compete in sports as diverse as snowboarding, figure skating, gymnastics, tennis and **luge**.

You may not know the meaning of the word *luge*. However, you can continue reading without worrying about the exact meaning because you observe other things:

- *Luge* is a word that is included in a list of sports;
- This is the only time the word *luge* is used in the reading.

As a result, you can probably guess that *luge* is a kind of sport that is mentioned only once in the reading. Therefore, you probably don't need to understand its exact meaning in order to continue reading. You must decide if the new word is important to understand, or if you can still understand the main points of the reading without knowing its exact meaning.

B. Discuss with the class how you can decide if it is important to understand the meaning of a word or not. Here are some clues.

CHARACTERISTICS OF A WORD THAT **IS NOT** IMPORTANT TO THE MEANING OF THE READING	CHARACTERISTICS OF A WORD THAT **IS** IMPORTANT TO THE MEANING OF THE READING
• The word isn't repeated often.	• The word is repeated frequently.
• The word is included in a list of examples.	• The word is included in the title or subheading(s) of a reading.
• The word is an adjective that you can guess is positive or negative.	• The word is highlighted in some way (in bold or italics) in the reading.

C. As you read the next article, use these strategies to help you with unfamiliar vocabulary.
- Guess the meaning of the word from its context.
- Guess the meaning of the word from its root word, or by removing its prefix or suffix.
- Decide if you can keep reading without knowing the exact meaning of the word.

VOCABULARY BUILD

A. Here are some words that will help you understand Reading 2. The part of speech is shown in parentheses next to each word (n. = noun; v. = verb; adj. = adjective). Check the words you understand. Then, check the words you use. If you don't know a word, leave the box blank.

	UNDERSTAND	USE		UNDERSTAND	USE
involved* (adj.) in	☐	☐	perspective* (n.)	☐	☐
specialization (n.)	☐	☐	burnout (n.)	☐	☐
deliberate (adj.)	☐	☐	acquisition* (n.) of	☐	☐
focus* (v.) on	☐	☐	elite (adj.)	☐	☐
implications* (n.) of	☐	☐	recreational (adj.)	☐	☐
emphasis* (n.) on	☐	☐	drill (n.)	☐	☐
diversification* (n.) of	☐	☐	coach (n.)	☐	☐
motor skills (n.)	☐	☐	acknowledge* (v.)	☐	☐

* Appears on the Academic Word List

B. Read each sentence and circle the word or phrase that best matches the meaning of the word(s) in bold. When you have finished, check your answers with a partner and confirm these with the class.

1 Many active adults report that they were **involved in** a broad range of organized sports during their youth.

a) tangled up in   b) interested in   c) implicated in

2 Early **specialization** in sport is often characterized by high amounts of practice and low amounts of play.

    a) limiting activities to only one   b) believing in activities   c) thinking about activities

3 Active children enjoy **deliberate** play activities to improve their fitness.

    a) accidental   b) unfortunate   c) planned and purposeful

4 Early specialization and an increased **focus on** practice activities during childhood can produce a champion.

    a) appreciation for   b) attention to   c) understanding of

5 Parents and coaches must consider the **implications of** early practice and training for a child.

    a) possible negative effects of   b) possible future effects of   c) possible positive effects of

6 Some coaches place too much **emphasis on** winning even if the child is unhappy.

    a) importance on   b) money on   c) fear about

7 Early **diversification of** sport activities is important to prevent injury.

    a) increase in the number of   b) drop in the intensity of   c) recognition of the importance of

8 One of the goals of youth-sport programs is the teaching of **motor skills**.

    a) car movements   b) complex muscle actions   c) talking ability

9 From a health **perspective**, too much early practice can cause physical problems in later life.

    a) concern   b) point of view   c) hope

10 Early specialization can lead to decreased enjoyment and to disappointment, discouragement and **burnout**, since young people may experience a sense of failure if they are unable to meet their goals.

    a) sad feeling from a shock   b) pleased feeling from success   c) tired feeling from overwork

11 Reducing the **acquisition of** sport skills to only practice fails to recognize important developmental, motivational and psychosocial aspects of human abilities.

    a) learning of   b) beginning of   c) effort of

12 Practice activities during the early years can be effective in producing **elite** performers.

    a) least competitive   b) worst prepared   c) most skilled

13 Some children are interested in playing **recreational** sports while others are motivated to pursue competitive sports.

    a) serious   b) successful   c) non-competitive

⑭ An example of a deliberate practice activity is a **drill**, like passing the soccer ball three times before shooting on the net.

   a) false start   b) repetition   c) accidental
                                   of an action   accomplishment

⑮ The role of a **coach** may change as athletes become more competitive.

   a) parent   b) friend   c) sport teacher

⑯ Most athletes **acknowledge** the support of their coaches and parents.

   a) recognize   b) are unhappy with   c) explain

C. Many of the nouns and verbs you just considered are not used alone as single words but used with prepositions (*in, of, on*). Find the best word + preposition combination in the box to fill in the blanks in the sentences that follow.

acquisition **of**	emphasis **on**	implications **of**	specialization **in**
diversification **of**	focus **on**	involved **in**	

❶ Although early _____ women's gymnastics is required to be competitive, success in that sport comes at a cost.

❷ Some coaches place an _____ good sportsmanship, leadership and self-discipline.

❸ The key to long-term success in sports is early _____ athletic activities.

❹ The _____ motor skills is one of the goals of youth-sport programs.

❺ While large numbers of children are _____ sports, only a small percentage of them remain active into adulthood.

❻ With health care costs rising, there is a strong _____ maintaining active participation in sports for life.

❼ The _____ an inactive lifestyle must be considered.

FOCUS ON READING

Scanning For Key Words

When you have a reading with a set of questions, reading the questions first can help you find the answers faster. If you identify key words in the questions, you can scan for these in the reading. Key words can help you locate the answers. Key words are often nouns that follow "what are" or "what is" in questions.

A. In this activity, key words are in bold in the questions. Read the questions first. Then, scan Reading 2 for the key words from the questions. Answer the questions in one or two sentences, and repeat the key words in your answer. The first one has been done for you as an example.

❶ What are the **three objectives of youth sport**?

   <u>The three objectives of youth sport are to improve physical health, develop psychosocial health</u>

   <u>(e.g., cooperation, discipline, leadership and self-control) and teach motor skills.</u>

2 When people develop youth-sport programs, what **implications must they consider**?

_____

_____

_____

3 What is more likely to happen if children and youth participate in **deliberate play or deliberate practice activities** during childhood?

_____

_____

_____

4 What are **deliberate play activities**? Give an example.

_____

_____

_____

5 What are **deliberate practice activities**? Give an example.

_____

_____

_____

6 What is **early specialization**?

_____

_____

_____

7 What is the **most effective way** to improve performance?

_____

_____

_____

8 From a health perspective, what may be the negative consequences of **an overemphasis on deliberate practice** at a young age?

_____

_____

_____

9 From a skill acquisition perspective, what are **the consequences of early specialization**?

_____

_____

_____

10 What is the danger of reducing the acquisition of sports skills to **deliberate practice only**?

_____

_____

_____

11 According to the authors, what is **the best way to achieve long-term health benefits**?

_____

_____

_____

12 What should be **the aim of sports programs** for all children and youth?

_____

_____

_____

B. When you have finished answering the questions, discuss your answers with another student.

Development of Youth Sport Programs

Objectives of Youth Sport

Youth sport has the potential to accomplish three important objectives in children's development. First, sport 5 programs provide youth with opportunities to be physically active, which can lead to improved physical health. Second, youth-sport programs have long been considered important to 10 youth's psychosocial development, providing opportunities to learn important life skills such as cooperation, discipline, leadership and self-control. Third, youth-sport programs are critical for the learning of motor skills; these motor skills serve as a foundation for future national sport stars and recreational adult- 15 sport participants. When coaches develop activities for youth practices and when sport organizations design youth-sport programs, they must consider ... the implications of deliberate play, deliberate practice and early specialization ...

Deliberate Play, Deliberate Practice and Early Specialization

Research from Telama, Hirvensalo and Raitakari (2006) states that regular participa- 20 tion in deliberate play or deliberate practice activities during childhood and youth (ages nine to eighteen) increases the likelihood of participation in sports during adulthood by six times for both males and females. Côté and colleagues (Côté & Hay, 2002; Côté, Baker, & Abernethy, 2003, 2007) define deliberate play activities in sport as those designed to maximize enjoyment. These activities are regulated by flexible rules 25 adapted from standardized sport rules and are set up by the children or by an involved adult. Children typically change rules to find a point where their game is similar to the actual sport but still allows for play at their level. For example, children may change soccer and basketball rules to suit their environment and their needs (e.g., playing in the street, on a playing field or in someone's backyard). When involved in deliberate 30 play activities, children are less concerned with the outcome of their behaviour (i.e., whether they win or lose) than with the behaviour (i.e., having fun). On the other hand, Ericsson, Krampe and Tesch-Römer (1993) suggest that the most effective learning occurs through involvement in highly structured activities defined as deliberate practice. Deliberate practice activities require effort, generate no immediate rewards, 35 and are motivated by the goal of improving performance rather than the goal of enjoyment. Early specialization is often characterized by high amounts of deliberate practice and low amounts of deliberate play. Early specialization is defined as limiting participation to one sport that is practised on a year-round basis ...

When individuals are involved in deliberate play, they experiment with new or dif- 40 ferent combinations of behaviours, but not necessarily in the most effective way to improve performance ... In contrast, when individuals are involved in deliberate practice, they exhibit behaviour focused on improving performance by the most effective means available. For example, the backhand skill in tennis could be learned and improved over time by playing matches or by creating fun practice situations.

45 However, players could more effectively improve their backhand performance by practising drills that might be considered less enjoyable. Although the drills used in deliberate practice might not be the most enjoyable, they might be the most relevant to improving performance. When one is considering the optimal amount of deliberate play, deliberate practice, and involvement in other sports that children should have 50 in their early years, one has to consider the three objectives of youth sport: health, psychosocial development and the learning of motor skills.

Early Specialization and Deliberate Practice Considerations

From a health perspective, an overemphasis on deliberate practice at a young age and early specialization can lead to dropout, muscle overuse, injury and athletes' 55 failure to develop transferable skills (Fraser-Thomas, Côté, & Deakin, 2008a). Early specialization often has harmful effects on emotional and psychological development, such as decreased enjoyment, disappointment, discouragement and burnout since youth may experience a sense of failure if they are unable to meet their goals after investing so heavily (Fraser-Thomas, Côté & Deakin, 2008b). Early specialization is 60 also a concern for youth's social development because it can lead to missed social opportunities experienced through early diversification (Wright & Côté, 2003).

From a skill-acquisition perspective, there is evidence that early specialization and an increased focus on deliberate practice activities during the early years can be effective in producing elite performers (Law, Côté & Ericsson, 2007); however, as 65 outlined above, there are many costs associated with this pattern of activities. It appears that deliberate play and involvement in various sporting activities may serve as a more cost-effective way for youth to explore their physical capacities in various contexts and to develop their sport skills. Analyses of elite athletes' early involvement in sports show that deliberate play activities and early diversification in sport activi-70 ties are important during the first few years of sport participation. For example, Soberlak and Côté (2003) showed that elite ice hockey players spent slightly more

time in deliberate play activities than deliberate practice activities before age twenty. Although much research sug-75 gests that involvement in deliberate practice is a consistent factor that differentiates elite from non-elite athletes (Helsen, Starkes, & Hodges, 1998), the difference of time invested in delib-80 erate practice activities generally occurs during the adolescent and adult years. Baker and Côté (2006) suggest that reducing the acquisition of sport skills to a single dimension (i.e., deliberate 85 practice) fails to acknowledge important developmental, motivational and psychosocial aspects of human abilities. However, the peak age in some sports, such as female gymnastics and 90 figure skating, tends to be quite young. Athletes in these sports are sometimes required to specialize early in order to reach the highest levels. In these programs, extreme caution should be used. Training programs must always consider children's physical, psychological, social and cognitive development.

95 Overall, early specialization and too much emphasis on deliberate practice activities during the early years of sport involvement may lead to health problems or withdrawal. Instead, an emphasis on various sport activities and deliberate play activities during childhood is likely to have immediate developmental and long-term health benefits.

Many youth-sport programs are designed to eventually expect specialization as ath-
100 letes age and mature. Although this is a path that many young athletes choose to follow, it is not a route for all youth. Given that a lot of research suggests adolescent sport withdrawal is a result of the required time commitment and competitive focus (Petlichkoff, 1993), sport programs should aim to offer both specialization (deliberate practice) and recreational programs (deliberate play) so that all adolescents can con-
105 tinue to enjoy and participate in sport.

References

Baker, J., & Côté, J. (2006). Shifting training requirements during athlete development: The relationship among deliberate practice, deliberate play and other sport involvement in the acquisition of sport expertise. In D. Hackfort, & G. Tenenbaum (Eds.), *Essential processes for attaining peak performance* (pp. 92–109). Aachen, Germany: Meyer and Meyer.

Côté, J., Baker, J., & Abernethy, B. (2003). From play to practice: A developmental framework for the acquisition of expertise in team sport. In J. Starkes, & K. A. Ericsson (Eds.), *Recent advances in research on sport expertise* (pp. 84–114). Champaign, IL: Human Kinetics.

Côté, J., Baker, J., & Abernethy, B. (2007). Practice and play in the development of sport expertise. In R. Eklund, & G. Tenenbaum (Eds.), *Handbook of sports psychology* (3rd ed., pp. 184–202). Hoboken, NJ: Wiley.

Côté, J., & Hay, J. (2002). Children's involvement in sport: A developmental perspective. In J.M. Silva III, & D.E. Stevens (Eds.), *Psychological foundations of sport* (pp. 78–87). Philadelphia, PA: American Society for Testing and Materials.

Ericsson, K. A., Krampe, R.T., & Tesch-Römer, C. (1993). The role of deliberate practice in the acquisition of expert performance. *Psychological Review, 100,* 363–406.

Fraser-Thomas, J., Côté, J., & Deakin, J. (2008a). Examining adolescent sport dropout and prolonged engagement from a developmental perspective. *Journal of Applied Sport Psychology, 20,* 318–333.

Fraser-Thomas, J., Côté, J., & Deakin, J. (2008b). Understanding dropout and prolonged engagement in adolescent competitive sport. *Psychology of Sport and Exercise, 9,* 645–662.

Helsen, W.F., Starkes, J.L., & Hodges, N.J. (1998). Team sports and the theory of deliberate practice. *Journal of Sport & Exercise Psychology, 20,* 12–34.

Law, M.P., Côté, J., & Ericsson, K.A. (2007). Characteristics of expert development in rhythmic gymnastics: A retrospective study. *International Journal of Sport and Exercise Psychology, 5,* 82–103.

Petlichkoff, L.M. (1993). Coaching children: Understanding the motivational process. *Sport Science Review, 2,* 48–61.

Soberlak, P., & Côté, J. (2003). Developmental activities of elite ice hockey players. *Journal of Applied Sport Psychology, 15,* 41–49.

Telama, R., Hirvensalo, M., & Raitakari, O. (2006). Participation in organized youth sport as a predictor of adult physical activity: A 21-year longitudinal study. *Paediatric Exercise Science, 17,* 76–88.

Wright, A.D., & Côté, J. (2003). A retrospective analysis of leadership development through sport. *The Sport Psychologist, 17,* 268–291.

Côté, J., & Fraser-Thomas, J. (2011). Youth involvement and positive development in sport. In P. Crocker (Ed.), *Sport and exercise psychology: A Canadian perspective* (2nd ed., pp. 229–255). Toronto, ON: Pearson.

Academic
Survival Skill

Using Citations and References

One of the key characteristics of academic writing is that it builds on the work of earlier authors. In 1159, John of Salisbury, an English writer, expressed this idea when he wrote that writers "stand on the shoulders of giants." Today, writers use citations and references to acknowledge the ideas of earlier authors in order to avoid plagiarizing. *Plagiarizing* is copying or using someone else's words or ideas without giving that person credit for them.

Look again at Reading 2. How do the writers show that their ideas are based on the ideas of earlier authors? You have probably noticed that there are two different ways of presenting the citations. Sometimes the parentheses go around only the year of publication; sometimes the parentheses go around the author's name and the year of publication.

A. Why is there a difference in how the authors write their citations?

_____

_____

B. Notice that the citations are short; the references are longer and contain more information.

1 Why are the citations short?

_____

_____

2 Why are the references at the end of the reading?

_____

_____

3 Each reference contains a lot of information. Why does the reader need so much information?

_____

_____

4 What kind of information is included in a reference?

_____

_____

_____

C. Most often, writers use citations when they want to recognize an earlier author for a statistic, a definition, or research that shows or proves something. The citations from paragraph 2 (lines 19–32) are listed below. For each citation, write the reason for the citation (a statistic, a definition or research) in the column beside it. Check your answers with the class.

CITATION	REASON FOR USING THE CITATION
Telama, Hirvensalo & Raitakari (2006)	_____: to show how important it is for children to participate in sports
(Côté & Hay, 2002; Côté, Baker, & Abernethy, 2003, 2007)	_____: of deliberate play
Ericsson, Krampe, and Tesch-Römer (1993)	_____: to show effective learning occurs with deliberate practice

D. Using academic citations and references accomplishes several of the authors' goals. Look at the list of these goals. With a partner, check two or three of the goals that you think are the most important. Discuss your choices with the class.
- To recognize the work of earlier authors
- To give credit to earlier authors
- To give the writing an academic look
- To avoid plagiarism
- To demonstrate the authors are familiar with research and their field of study

FOCUS ON WRITING

Improving Your Writing with Specific Vocabulary

You can quickly improve your written and spoken English by selecting specific and descriptive vocabulary. This will allow your readers and listeners to "see" your exact meaning. However, selecting better vocabulary is more than just useful for academic writing—it is *essential*. Academic writing is used to express complex ideas. If you use words that are not specific, your reader may not understand your exact meaning.

You do not need to spend a lot of time looking in a dictionary or a thesaurus to find better vocabulary. Think of words that you already recognize but have yet to use. The words don't have to be long or complicated. Spend time searching your mind for better words; consult a dictionary or thesaurus only as a last resort.

Look at these sentences that coaches might say to their athletes. The words in bold indicate non-specific and inaccurate verbs, adjectives and nouns.

Example: If you **do** these recommendations, you will **get** success.
With better vocabulary:
    If you **follow** these recommendations, you will **achieve** success.
    If you **accomplish** these recommendations, you will **attain** success.

Example: You can **do better** in swimming if you **work** when you are **very tired**.
With better vocabulary:
    You can **improve** in swimming if you **train** when you are **exhausted**.
    You can **increase your endurance** if you **swim** when you are **fatigued**.

Now look at these sentences that athletes might say to their coaches. Work with another student to identify the words that are non-specific, and then select better verbs, adjectives and nouns.

1 I will work hard to get the goal.

2 The work is very difficult and the pressure is too much.

3 There are some bad things about training so much.

WARM-UP ASSIGNMENT
Write a Short Answer

In many of your classes, you will be asked to respond in writing to questions with short answers. Short answers can be as brief as one or two sentences or as long as half a page, depending on the content. In order to write a successful short answer, you will need to follow these steps:

• Review what you know and decide on the content that you want to include in your short answer.

• Organize your content in a recognizable way—from simple to complex, in chronological order or from beginning to end. Your challenge is to organize the information so that it is not only brief but also logically presented.

• Repeat key words from the question in the first line of your answer.

• Select accurate and specific vocabulary.

Refer to the section on short answers in the Models Chapter (page 178) to see some examples of short answers and to learn more about how to write them.

Write short answers to the following questions.

1 You are planning a youth-sport program. What are your goals for the program and why?

2 You are a coach for a children's soccer team. What kind of activities will you plan and why?

> When you receive feedback from your teacher or your class-mates on this Warm-Up Assignment, you will have some information that you can use to improve your writing on the Final Assignment.

VOCABULARY BUILD

A. Check the words you understand. Then, check the words you use.

	UNDERSTAND	USE		UNDERSTAND	USE
colleagues* (n.)	☐	☐	motivated (adj.)	☐	☐
trajectories (n.)	☐	☐	reciprocal (adj.)	☐	☐
sample (n.)	☐	☐	oriented* (adj.)	☐	☐
embark (v.) on	☐	☐	overuse (adj.)	☐	☐
commit* (v.) to	☐	☐	peak (adj.)	☐	☐
primarily* (adv.)	☐	☐	role* (n.)	☐	☐

* Appears on the Academic Word List

B. Guess the meaning of the words in bold in each of the following sentences. When you have finished, match each word to a definition from the list that follows. Write the letter corresponding to the correct definition in the space provided. Confirm your answers with the class.

1. The Developmental Model of Sport Participation (DMSP) by Côté and **colleagues** (Côté et al., 2007) emerged from extensive interviews with athletes in a variety of sports: hockey, baseball, gymnastics, rowing, tennis and triathlon. _____

2. The DMSP proposes three possible sport participation **trajectories**: (1) recreational participation through sampling, (2) elite performance through sampling and (3) elite performance through early specialization. _____

3. The years between the ages of six and twelve are called the **sampling** years. During these years, children should have the opportunity to **sample** a wide variety of sports. They will learn the habit of active living through **sampling**. _____

4. After the sampling years, sport participants can choose to either stay involved in sport at a recreational level (recreational years, age thirteen plus) or **embark on** a path that focuses primarily on performance (ages thirteen to fifteen; investment years, age sixteen plus). _____

5. During the investment years, youth **commit to** only one activity and participate **primarily** in deliberate practice. (commit to) _____; (primarily) _____

6. It is important that young athletes who specialize early in their sport careers be **motivated**. Unfortunately, some early specializers are pushed into performing by their parents or coaches. _____

7. During both the specializing and the investment years, a more **reciprocal** coach-athlete respect develops, with coaches' styles becoming more skill **oriented** and technical. (reciprocal) _____; (oriented) _____

8. In addition, early specializers often experience **overuse** injuries. _____

9. In sports where **peak** performance is achieved before puberty (e.g., women's gymnastics, figure skating), early specialization is often necessary to reach elite performance. _____

10. Essentially, parents progress from a leadership **role** during the sampling years to a following and support **role** during the specializing and investment years (Côté, 1999). _____

a) possible paths to achieve a goal	**g)** mutual; where two people do or give the same things to each other
b) decide to use their time to achieve a goal	**h)** resulting from too much use
c) expected participation; influence	**i)** mainly
d) excited to do something interesting	**j)** highest or best
e) people you work with	**k)** start something new
f) trying an activity to see what it is like	**l)** giving a lot of time or effort to something

Identifying Key Words in Questions

As with the previous reading, look at the questions first. With a partner, identify the key words in each question. Then, scan the reading for the key words from the questions.

1 What are the three possible trajectories for young athletes participating in sport as defined by the Developmental Model of Sport Participation (DMSP)?

_____

_____

_____

2 What are the ages the authors define as ...

a) the foundation years? _____

b) the recreational years? _____

c) the specialization years? _____

d) the investment years? _____

3 What are the key characteristics of the athlete experience (at each age) in each of the three trajectories?

_____

_____

_____

_____

_____

_____

_____

_____

_____

_____

_____

_____

_____

4 Which trajectories do Simon Whitfield, Mary Lou Retton and Scott Bradshaw represent?

Simon Whitfield: _____

Mary Lou Retton: _____

Scott Bradshaw: _____

The Developmental Model of Sport Participation

The Developmental Model of Sport Participation (DMSP) by Côté and colleagues (Côté et al., 2007) emerged from extensive
5 interviews with athletes in a variety of sports, such as hockey, baseball, gymnastics, rowing, tennis and triathlon. The DMSP proposes three possible sport
10 participation trajectories: (1) recreational participation through sampling, (2) elite performance through sampling and (3) elite performance through early specialization. Two of these trajectories, recreational participation and elite performance through sampling, have the
15 same foundation from ages six to twelve. After the sampling years, sport participants can choose to either stay involved in sport at a recreational level (recreational years, age thirteen plus) or embark on a path that focuses primarily on performance (specializing years, ages thirteen to fifteen; investment years, age sixteen plus). These two trajectories have different outcomes in terms of performance but similar psychosocial and physical
20 health benefits. A third possible trajectory consists of elite performance through early specialization. Although this trajectory leads to elite performance, it can also result in reduced physical health (i.e., overuse injuries) and enjoyment.

Trajectory 1: Recreational Participation through Sampling

During the sampling years (ages six to twelve), athletes participate in a variety of
25 sports with the focus being primarily on deliberate play activities. These years are considered essential building blocks for recreational sport participation. The recreational years (age thirteen plus) are usually seen as an extension of the sampling years, with the primary goals being enjoyment and health. Activities can involve deliberate play and deliberate practice, and sport programs are flex-
30 ible enough to adapt to individual interests and ages. During the sampling and recreational years, coaches are primarily kind, supportive and encouraging (McCarthy & Jones, 2007). Parents' roles include introducing their children to sports, enrolling their children in diverse activities, and providing their children with necessary resources and equipment.

35 Trajectory 2: Elite Performance through Sampling

For youth interested in a more performance-oriented path, a second trajectory of the DMSP suggests that specialization begins around age thirteen, after the sampling years. The specializing years (ages thirteen to fifteen) are seen as a transitional stage to the investment years (age sixteen plus). During the specializing years, youth
40 engage in fewer activities, which are a mix of deliberate play and deliberate practice activities; during the investment years, youth commit to only one activity and participate primarily in deliberate practice. During both the specializing and the investment years, a more reciprocal coach-athlete respect develops, with coaches' styles becoming more skill oriented and technical. Parents become less involved but

[45] provide more financial and emotional support by helping their children through challenges and obstacles. Essentially, parents progress from a leadership role during the sampling years to a following and support role during the specializing and investment years (Côté, 1999).

Trajectory 3: Elite Performance through Early Specialization

[50] In sports where peak performance is achieved before puberty (e.g., women's gymnastics, figure skating), early specialization is often necessary to reach elite performance. Elite performers in these early-specialization sports usually skip the sampling years and, consequently, do not always experience the most positive psychosocial development. In addition, early specializers often experience overuse injuries. The [55] early specialization path is characterized by high amounts of deliberate practice and low amounts of deliberate play in a context that focuses on performance.

Other Trajectories

Opportunities for horizontal movement across stages (e.g., going from investment to recreational) should be provided for participants so that individuals can change [60] their level of participation at any age if they so desire. Unfortunately, in many sports it is difficult for a sixteen-year-old adolescent to invest in a sport if he or she has not been specializing in that sport since approximately age thirteen; however, in some sports, such as triathlon, investment in adulthood is possible (Baker, Côté, & Deakin, 2005). Finally, at any stage of development, youth may also choose to [65] disengage from sport and physical activity altogether. If this is the case, their youth-sport programs clearly failed to achieve the first objective of youth-sport programming: the long term physical health of participants. Unfortunately, many youth-sport programs are failing to reach this objective, as evidenced by current adolescent and adult inactivity rates.

References

Baker, J., Côté, J., & Deakin, J. (2005). Expertise in ultra-endurance triathletes: Early sport involvement, training structure, and the theory of deliberate practice. *Journal of Applied Sport Psychology*, *17*, 64–78.

Côté, J. (1999). The influence of the family in the development of talent in sport. *The Sport Psychologist*, *13*, 395–417.

Côté, J., Baker, J., & Abernethy, B. (2007). Practice and play in the development of sport expertise. In R. Eklund & G. Tenenbaum (Eds.), *Handbook of sports psychology* (3rd ed., pp. 184–202). Hoboken, NJ: Wiley.

McCarthy, P.J., & Jones, M.V. (2007). A qualitative study of sport enjoyment in the sampling years. *The Sport Psychologist*, *21*, 400–416.

———

Côté, J., & Fraser-Thomas, J. (2011). Youth involvement and positive development in sport. In P. Crocker (Ed.), *Sport and exercise psychology: A Canadian perspective* (2nd ed., pp. 245–255). Toronto, ON: Pearson.

FOCUS ON WRITING

Introducing Examples into a Text

In academic writing, it is important to include examples to support a point or provide more information to the reader. Writers introduce examples with specific phrases or abbreviations:

- for example
- e.g., = *exempli gratia*, which means "for example" in Latin
- such as
- i.e., = *id est*, which means "that is" in Latin

A. There are conventions about how to introduce examples in academic writing. The best phrase or abbreviation to use depends on the position of the example in the sentence. Complete the table and answer the questions that follow to find out how these expressions are used. When you have finished, confirm your answers with the class.

	PHRASE OR ABBREVIATION	POSITION IN SENTENCE: BEGINNING OR MID-SENTENCE	IN PARENTHESES: YES OR NO
READING 2			
LINE 27	For example, children may change ...	beginning	no
LINE 28	... (e.g., playing in the street, ...)		
LINE 30	... (i.e., whether they win or lose) ...		
LINE 31	... (i.e., having fun) ...		
LINE 43	For example, the backhand skill in tennis ...		
LINE 56	... development, such as decreased enjoyment, ...		
LINE 70	For example, Soberlak and Côté (2003) showed that ...		
LINE 84	... (i.e., deliberate practice) ...		
READING 3			
LINE 5	... sports, such as hockey, baseball, ...		
LINE 21	... (i.e., overuse injuries) ...		
LINE 50	... (e.g., women's gymnastics, figure skating), ...		
LINE 58	... (e.g., going from investment to recreational) ...		
LINE 89	... sports, such as triathlon, investment ...		

❶ In which sentence position are the abbreviations *e.g.*, and *i.e.*, used? What punctuation is used? Are they in parentheses?

_____

_____

❷ In which sentence position is *such as* used to introduce examples? Is *such as* in parentheses? What punctuation is used?

_____

_____

❸ When is *for example* used and with what punctuation?

_____

_____

B. Use the correct phrase or abbreviation in the blanks of this paragraph to introduce the examples. Pay careful attention to punctuation.

In some sports, _____ women's gymnastics and figure skating, athletes

need to specialize early. However, in other sports (_____ triathlon), elite

athletes are usually comparatively older. Cross-country skiers, _____

Canadian Beckie Scott, are good examples of this. Most athletes who pursue

their sports into the investment years train with coaches. _____

Simon Whitfield trained in Australia with a variety of coaches before he won his

gold medal. All elite athletes worry about hurting themselves (_____ overuse

injuries) while training. Athletes who have spent their early years playing

a variety of sports, and who specialize at a later age, may be less likely to

experience injury.

C. Return to the second Focus on Reading (page 10), questions 4 and 5. These questions asked you to give examples in your answers. If necessary, rewrite those answers using one of these methods to introduce your examples.

❶ _____

_____

❷ _____

_____

FINAL ASSIGNMENT
Write a Short Answer Test

Use this short answer test to help you prepare for assignments, tests and exams that you must write in your other classes. Refer to the Models Chapter (page 178) to see an example of a short answer and to learn more about how to write one.

Complete all the questions in one hour. Write the answers in your notebook or on a separate sheet of paper. Plan carefully so that you don't run out of time at the end of the test period. Leave some time to proofread your answers.

Use specific vocabulary and include examples (using the methods you learned) to support your points.

❶ What are some of the negative consequences that early sport specializers may experience?

❷ Briefly describe the three trajectories that young athletes might experience.

❸ How do the roles of parents and coaches change as athletes get older?

❹ In your opinion, which is the best trajectory for an athlete, and why?

CHAPTER 2

A Fitting Education

Going to college or university is becoming an increasingly common experience for young adults around the world. However, there are many different institutions of higher education, and selecting the one that best fits a student's needs can be challenging.

How do students decide where and what to study? How do their decisions fit with enrolment trends in Canada?

In this chapter, you will

- discuss academic choices and learn about enrolment trends at Canadian colleges and universities;

- use vocabulary related to school and program selection, and trends in education;

- learn how to skim a text for general comprehension;

- learn characteristics of various types of text in order to read more efficiently;

- apply knowledge of sentence structure to describe numerical and statistical information;

- learn correct question format and use it to design a survey and collect information;

- write a report based on the data you collect with your survey.

GEARING UP

A. With a small group of students, discuss why you decided to attend your college or university. Some of you may have travelled from another country to pursue your education. If so, why did you choose to study in this country?

B. In the following table, write the name of each student in your group and take notes about the factors that influenced his or her decisions.

STUDENT'S NAME	FACTORS THAT INFLUENCED HIS OR HER DECISIONS

Colleges, Universities and Academic Programs

A. Read this short description of the differences between universities and colleges in Canada. When you have finished, complete the table in the Vocabulary Build using the vocabulary in bold from the reading.

B. Then, with a classmate, discuss which institution and program you want to study in (or are studying in) and your long term goal. Use the key vocabulary from the reading and table.

What Is the Difference Between a University and a College?

Universities are educational institutions that students attend after at least twelve years of school, or after **secondary school**, for studies leading to a **certificate** or **degree** (e.g., **bachelor's**, **master's**, **doctorate**). All Association of Universities and Colleges of
5 Canada (AUCC) member universities offer three- or four-year bachelor's degree pro-

grams; most offer one- to three-year master's degree programs and a number also offer doctoral or Ph.D. programs (three years or more). Bach-
10 elor's degree programs are **under-graduate programs**; master's and Ph.D. degrees are called **graduate level programs**. Some universities are called **institutes**, **university colleges**
15 or **schools**.

Public colleges may also be known as **institutes of technology**, **community colleges**, **polytechnics**, **colleges of applied arts and technology**
20 and, in Quebec, Collèges d'enseignement général et professionnel (**CEGEPs**). They offer a wide range of educational programs in a vast array of technical and professional fields, taking anywhere from a few months to four years to complete. The Quebec CEGEPs offer two streams of education: three-year **vocational** and two-year **pre-university** programs. In addition, some colleges in Canada provide programs
25 that prepare students to transfer into universities with advanced standing, some offer joint **diplomas** and degrees with university partners, many others offer academic and **applied degrees**, and an increasing number are now offering **post-graduate diplomas**.

———

AUCC. (2010). Notes for international students. Retrieved from: http://www.aucc.ca/media-room/publications/notes-for-international-students

VOCABULARY BUILD

DESCRIPTION	VOCABULARY FROM READING
school you attend when you are fourteen to seventeen years old	secondary school

▶

DESCRIPTION	VOCABULARY FROM READING
schools you attend as an adult to learn a trade	
what you earn when you finish college	
schools you attend as an adult to learn an academic subject	
what you earn when you finish university	
first degree from a university	
second degree from a university	
third degree from a university	
what you study for when you finish a university degree and decide to study next at a college	
program of study in a Quebec CEGEP to learn a trade	
program of study in a Quebec CEGEP to prepare for university	
program that you study at a college before you transfer to a university	
program of study for a bachelor's degree	
program of study for a master's or Ph.D. degree	

Skimming to Gather Information about a Text

When you skim a text, you look the text over quickly to determine
- how long it is, because you want to know how much time it will take to read;
- what type of text it is, because you want to know what method of organization the author used;
- who wrote it, because the author may have a unique perspective on the topic;
- when it was written, because you want to know if it is older or more recent;
- the main topic, because (of course) you want to know what you are reading about;
- the main points, because it is helpful to have an idea about what the author is going to say before you begin to read more closely.

Most of this information you can discover from simply looking at the text. However, it may be more difficult to discover the main points of a text. To skim for the main points in a reading, you should quickly read
- the title;
- any subheadings;
- any captions for pictures or charts;
- the introduction;
- the first sentence of each paragraph;
- the conclusion.

READING ②

Finding the Right Fit

A. Skim Reading 2 to find key information about the text.

1 How long is it? _____

2 What type of text is it? _____

3 Which clues help you identify the text type? _____

_____

_____

4 Who wrote it? _____

5 Who is the author interviewing and what is that person's profession?

_____

_____

6 When was it written? _____

7 What is the topic? _____

_____

8 What are the main points? _____

_____

_____

_____

How Do I Choose the Right Program for Me?
by Erin Millar

Simon Fraser University registrar says you don't necessarily have to decide on a career before you begin your studies: "An undergraduate degree is an undergraduate degree."

5 *There are many specialized programs to suit tangible career goals out there. What makes a good program? How can you wade through a university's marketing material to find out whether a program is for you?* Maclean's *chatted with Kate Ross, Registrar and Senior Director of Student Enrolment at Simon Fraser University, to find out.*

KATE ROSS: My philosophy is that an undergraduate degree is an undergraduate degree.
10 In some respects, employers don't really care what area it's from but it sends a message about capability. You probably have good analytical skills; you have writing ability; you have the ability to critically think. To some extent, it's not about what you took, but what you gained from it.

I think sometimes that young people think that they have to have a direction. They're
15 supposed to be able to say, "Well, I'm going to be an x."

But if somebody had told me when I did my undergraduate degree, that I would be in the role that I'm in now, I would have told them they were crazy.

I think we have come to a point where we get so tied to thinking we have to have a career, and we have to define what that career is, that it freezes us. I've told so
20 many students: just pick something that you like to start and let that potentially unfold for you.

Be open to trying different things so that something can emerge.

Learning what you don't like to do is almost as important as learning what you like to do. Part of the difficulty is that there is so much choice now. That is partly why
25 people don't know what they want to do or they don't know how to decide.

There are all sorts of things like dual degrees. Simon Fraser has a dual degree with a university in China and you can actually get a degree from both institutions in about five years in the computing science area.

So there's all of these different ways that you can do things
30 now that didn't exist before. My feeling is that you need to stay open to the possibilities.

ERIN MILLAR, *MACLEAN'S*: What if I don't know what I want to do, but I know I want to go to university?

KR: The key is to pick a university or an institution that
35 you think fits with you. Do you know if you are someone who can manage yourself in a very large place? Would you be more comfortable in a smaller institution? Think about what the campus life is like, if that is important to you. What kinds of opportunities exist that are academic but
40 are also about providing you with a more well-rounded education? If residence is important to you, what's residence like? What's the academic philosophy of the institution? Are they focused on ensuring that by the time you graduate you are going to be a well-rounded, capable graduate?

45 **EM:** How can a student find out if a program is actually any good?

KR: A student really needs to take the opportunity to talk to a program director or a faculty advisor. Ask them for names of recent graduates that you could talk to, to learn what their experience was like. Find out if there is a student association for each program. Look for programs that have an active student association because
50 that tells you something about students being engaged. Let's say you're going to be a business student in accounting. Do they have an active student group and does that student group have ties to external bodies like Certified Management Accountants? So particularly when you are looking for a very specialized program, really look for those types of things.

55 **EM:** All universities have slick marketing and promise the world with their programs. But what really makes a good program?

KR: First of all, I think the most important thing is that it is something that you have an interest and passion in. So I would even take a step back there and ask, are you really interested in it? Can you get excited about it? What might be a good
60 program for one person is not a good program for another.

I think you should look for relevance. Is there academic rigour in the program? Does it have breadth and depth? Does it challenge you to develop beyond your capabilities and beyond capabilities that you might not even know that you have? Does it give the opportunity for any kind of experiential learning? Are there co-op
65 opportunities? Are there international exchange opportunities? The kind of things that will really add to your undergraduate education. The one thing I haven't covered is costs.

What will I learn? How satisfied have past graduates been with the program? What can I do with this degree? Both for work and further schooling opportunities. For some people, that is actually where their head is. They are looking for a further academic experience at a graduate level. So ask what other further schooling opportunities exist.

Flexibility is another consideration. Can I take a year off? Can I take a term off? That's important for a lot of students now. Can I take some time off and come back fairly easily?

...

EM: If you take a specialized program, do you run the risk of ending up with a limited education that could lead to narrowed job opportunities?

KR: I don't think so. The only thing that could happen ... let's say you decided you want to do accounting and you got to your fourth year and you had never done a co-op program so you had actually never worked in an accounting office. And you got into an accounting office and you thought, "Oh no, I can't stand this." Then it might be harder to make a lateral move.

Think about the transferable skills that you gain from anything that you do, whether it's work or whether it's school, and think about what you can actually apply to another opportunity. Always think in regards to what are the transferable skills you have and help an employer understand those.

EM: Is there an advantage to attending a university for a career-focused or applied program, as opposed to going to a technical or vocational college?

KR: Think about what's the right place for you to start. For some students, they need the confidence building of being in a smaller institution that they can transfer from to get to university later. That's a really good place for some students because they may not have felt so confident in terms of their ability and then they have some success and they realize that they are more capable than they thought.

The other thing is that for some people, what they really want to do are trades.

EM: How can a student learn about co-op and internship opportunities? How do these help students transition into the workforce?

KR: I think that they are absolutely critical. They help students integrate theory and practice. They help students recognize and gain confidence in what they are learning when they can start to see that emerge in their abilities outside the classroom. I think that in most co-op programs, students end up in gaining that kind of experience that makes them more competent even when they come back to school. It also helps them focus their interest. It helps them figure out what they really want to do.

EM: Anything else you would like to add?

KR: The final thing would be to do something that you love. Go with what feels right. Be open to other opportunities at your institution. Focus on all of the other things that university offers including the student paper, clubs and so on.

Millar, Erin. (May 22, 2007). How do I choose the right program for me? *Maclean's*. Retrieved from: http://oncampus.macleans.ca/education/2007/05/22/how-do-i-choose-the-right-program-for-me/

B. Read the following questions, and use your scanning skills from Chapter 1, Focus on Reading (page 9) to find the answers in the interview. When you have finished, share your answers with a classmate and then discuss them with the class.

1 Kate Ross, the Registrar at Simon Fraser University, says, "An undergraduate degree is an undergraduate degree." What does she mean?

_____

_____

2 a) Which skills do you develop in an undergraduate degree, according to Ross?

_____

_____

b) Are there other important skills for an undergraduate student to develop?

_____

_____

3 Why does Ross believe that it can be hard for students to pick a study program?

_____

_____

4 What advice does she give to students who are worried about picking a career?

_____

_____

5 Do you think this is good advice? Explain your answer.

_____

_____

6 a) Ross suggests there are many factors students should consider before they pick a university program. List as many of these factors as you can.

_____

_____

_____

_____

b) In the Gearing Up section, you and your classmates discussed the factors that you considered when choosing an academic program. List factors from your discussion that were not mentioned in this interview.

_____

_____

_____

_____

7 Does Ross believe that universities or colleges are better? How do you know?

_____

_____

8 How can co-op or internship opportunities help students in the future?

_____

_____

9 What is Ross' final advice for students choosing a study program?

_____

_____

_____

Academic
Survival Skill

Asking Questions Using Correct Word Order

As you read in the interview with the Registrar from Simon Fraser University, writing and asking questions are essential skills that will help you find important information. During your years of study, you will need to ask questions of other students, teaching assistants, instructors and professors. When you write and ask questions, it is important to use correct question format as this will increase your confidence, as well as your chances of being understood and of receiving the information that you need.

Although it may be hard at first, don't be afraid to ask other students or teachers for help. Remember that it is easy for other students to help you, and it is the teachers' job to provide you with the information that you need. A good way to ask for information is to say "Excuse me" and then ask your question. Don't forget to smile. Students and teachers will be glad to help you.

Yes/No Questions

Generally, for questions with simple _yes_ or _no_ answers, an auxiliary verb (_to be_, _to have_, _to do_) or a modal auxiliary (_can_, _could_, _may_, _might_, _must_, _shall_, _should_, _will_, _would_) precedes the subject of the sentence. The main verb follows the subject of the sentence.

AUXILIARY (BE/HAVE/DO)	SUBJECT	MAIN VERB	REST OF SENTENCE
Is	he	enjoying	his studies?
Have	you	benefitted	from your education?
Does	the government	fund	higher education in your country?

MODAL AUXILIARY	SUBJECT	MAIN VERB (BASE FORM)	REST OF SENTENCE
Can	you	recommend	the best professor?
Should	sports	be	part of the curriculum?
Would	your parents	approve	of that school?

▶

An exception to this yes/no question pattern is when the verb *to be* is the main verb of the sentence. Then your questions look like this:

VERB *BE*	SUBJECT	REST OF SENTENCE
Was	she	happy at school?
Is	he	interested in his studies?
Were	they	well-informed about their school choices?

When you ask a question that has a yes/no answer, raise the pitch of your voice at the end of the question.

Information Questions

Generally, for questions that request information, a question word (*what, where, why, when, who, how*) is followed by either
• an auxiliary (*be/have/do*) or;
• a modal auxiliary (*can, could, may, might, must, shall, should, will, would*).

These are followed by the subject and main verb of the sentence.

QUESTION WORD	AUXILIARY/ MODAL AUXILIARY	SUBJECT	MAIN VERB	REST OF SENTENCE
What	did	you	study	at university?
Why	are	so many students	failing	first-year courses?
How	should	the government	support	higher education?

An exception to this information question pattern is when the verb *to be* is the main verb of the sentence. Then your questions look like this:

QUESTION WORD	*BE* (MAIN VERB)	SUBJECT	REST OF SENTENCE
Who	are	they?	
When	is	our next English class?	
Why	am	I	so tired after class?

Another exception to the pattern is *who* questions that elicit an answer that is the subject of the corresponding sentence.

QUESTION WORD	MAIN VERB	SUBJECT
Who	understood	the lecture? (Nobody understood the lecture.)
Who	took	calculus last semester? (Saroj and Raoul took calculus.)

When you ask a question that requires information, do not raise the pitch of your voice at the end of the question.

A. Working with two other students and using some of the ideas from Gearing Up and Reading 1, think of six (or more) questions you would like to ask your classmates about their reasons for coming to your college or university. Use the question formats you have learned to help you write accurate questions on a separate sheet of paper. Your teacher will review your questions to make sure you are using correct format.

B. Once your teacher has checked your questions, write them in the left-hand column of the following table. Then, write the names of the two other students at the top of the columns to the right.

C. Take turns asking and answering the questions. Practise raising your pitch for yes/no questions or keeping your pitch level at the end of information questions. As you listen to your classmate's responses, write brief, point-form notes in the columns under his or her name.

	QUESTION	NAME _____	NAME _____
1			
2			
3			
4			
5			
6			

D. After completing the table, select the most interesting piece of information you discovered and discuss it with the class.

WARM-UP ASSIGNMENT

Write a Short Report

Use the information you collected from your classmates about why they chose to study at your institution, and write a short two-page report.

Your report should include an introduction and sections on methods, results and discussion. Refer to the Models Chapter (page 181) to see an example of a report and to learn more about how to write one.

When you receive feedback from your teacher or classmates on this Warm-Up Assignment, you will have some information that you can use to improve your performance on your Final Assignment.

FOCUS ON WRITING

Using Varied Sentence Structure

Understanding basic sentence structure makes it easier to move on to more complex language tasks such as paraphrasing and summarizing. Simple sentences are the building blocks of writing. After you learn how to write simple sentences, you can make your writing more interesting by combining simple sentences in various ways.

A simple sentence expresses a full thought. It consists of an independent clause (IC) that includes a subject and a verb.

An IC can be very short or it can have two or more subjects and verbs.

> Example: Students study. (Full thought; subject + verb)
> Marina and Olga study and work during the day.
> (Full thought; two subjects + two verbs)

Here are some patterns that you can use to combine independent clauses to make your writing more interesting.

Pattern 1: Combine a *phrase* with an IC.

A phrase is a group of words that belong together to create meaning, but that do not contain a subject + verb combination. Examples of phrases are:
- in 2012
- at the end of the day
- with her decision

phrase + comma + IC	**In 2012,** he decided to study at university.
	At the end of the day, Hiromi was exhausted.
	Hoping to improve his career options, he decided to study at college.
IC + phrase	She was an undergraduate student **in her hometown**.
	Her parents were not happy **with her decision**.
	Paola wanted to study close **to her parents' home**.

Pattern 2: Combine a *dependent clause* (DC) with an IC.

A DC expresses an incomplete thought. It begins with a subordinate conjunction and includes a subject and a verb. Examples of dependent clauses are:
• when she started
• since exercise is important
• before the instructor assigned the homework

DC + comma + IC	**When she started,** she was a good student.
	After Xi finished the exam, she went home to sleep.
	Since exercise is important, sports should be part of a school's curriculum.
IC + DC (no comma)	She was a good student **when she started**.
	Mohammed registered early for classes **although he didn't know anyone else in the school**.
	He left the lecture **before the instructor assigned the homework**.

Here is a list of some of the more common subordinate conjunctions and their functions.

SUBORDINATE CONJUNCTION	FUNCTION	SUBORDINATE CONJUNCTION	FUNCTION
after/before	To establish a sequence	if/unless	To set a condition
although/even if/ even though	To present opposing ideas	since/when	To refer to a point in time
as/just as	To make a comparison	where/wherever	To introduce a place
as long as	To introduce a period of time	whether	To introduce a choice
because	To give a reason	while	To show simultaneous actions

Practising Sentence Patterns 1 and 2

1 On a separate sheet of paper, write four sentences. Two sentences should include phrases at the beginning or end of an independent clause and two sentences should include dependent clauses joined to independent clauses.

2 When you have finished, exchange your sentences with another student. Can you recognize the sentence combinations written by your partner?

3 Help each other correct any errors.

Pattern 3: Combine an IC with an IC using a *coordinate conjunction*.

When combining independent clauses, a comma is inserted before the coordinate conjunction.

IC + comma + coordinate conjunction + IC	She was a good student, **and** she worked hard.
	She was a good student, **but** she didn't like her teachers.
	She was a good student, **so** she reviewed her notes after every class.

Here is a list of coordinate conjunctions and their functions.

COORDINATE CONJUNCTION	FUNCTION	COORDINATE CONJUNCTION	FUNCTION
and	To add	or	To show an alternative
but	To contrast	so	To show a result
for	To introduce a reason	yet	To introduce two opposing ideas
nor	To add an idea after a negative statement		

Pattern 4: Combine an IC with an IC using a *semicolon (;)*.

Use a semicolon between two independent clauses when the meanings of the clauses are very close.

IC + semicolon + IC	He was a good student; he always had good study habits.
	The essay was long and complicated; there was too much information to organize.

Pattern 5: Combine two ICs using a *semicolon* and an *adverbial conjunction*.

In these cases, a comma is used after an adverbial conjunction.

IC + semicolon + adverbial conjunction + comma + IC	He was a good student; **however,** he became sick.
	He was a good student; **consequently,** he received high marks.

Here is a list of some of the more common adverbial conjunctions and their functions.

ADVERBIAL CONJUNCTION	FUNCTION	ADVERBIAL CONJUNCTION	FUNCTION
accordingly/ as a result/ consequently	To show a result	indeed/in fact	To emphasize

ADVERBIAL CONJUNCTION	FUNCTION	ADVERBIAL CONJUNCTION	FUNCTION
also/furthermore/moreover	To add	likewise/similarly	To show similarity
for example/for instance	To introduce an example	meanwhile/at the same time	To show simultaneous actions
however/nevertheless	To contrast	otherwise	To show an alternative consequence

Adding Interest by Using a Variety of Sentence Patterns

You now know five different ways to join independent clauses to other phrases and clauses.

1. Read the following paragraphs. They have been written using only independent clauses. Writing like this is grammatically correct but boring to read.

2. Working with another student, use your knowledge of how to combine independent clauses to make these paragraphs more interesting. Please note that there will be many correct answers.

> Quohong and Peter were students in a university writing course. They were worried. They had heard that academic writing was different in different countries. They had heard that copying information in this country was not allowed. Using ideas from another writer without identifying the writer was not permitted. These things were called *plagiarism*. Plagiarism was not acceptable at this university. Students who plagiarized could be punished.
>
> Their teacher carefully explained how to avoid plagiarism. They could use three methods. They could use quotes and reference the source of the quotes. They could paraphrase a source. They could summarize a source. For paraphrasing and summarizing, they either needed a reference or not. Unique research results or statistics required a reference. Information that was common knowledge did not require a reference. They felt better. They knew how to avoid plagiarism. They were ready to write their first essay.

FOCUS ON READING

Considering the Characteristics of a Text

When you read, it is helpful to know what type of text you are reading: a textbook, course notes, a magazine article, a newspaper story, a report, an essay, an e-mail, a website or a novel. Each type of text has different characteristics including purpose, organization, language and key features, and these characteristics may change how you approach the reading.

A. Read the information in the following table. Some of the boxes have been left blank. As a class, discuss what information should be added to the blank boxes.

TYPE OF TEXT	CHARACTERISTICS OF TEXT	HOW TO READ EFFICIENTLY
TEXTBOOK	• Provides information. • Content is organized under chapter titles, headings and subheadings. • Usually contains a table of contents and an index. • Sometimes key words or concepts are defined in text boxes in the margins. • May contain in-text citations and references. • Language is formal.	• In each chapter, skim to learn the topic and main points. • Scan to look for specific details. • Highlight important information.
COURSE NOTES	• Provides information. • Content is organized by topic or date. • Usually includes key information. • May leave some information out so students are required to complete the notes as they listen to the lecture. • Language is most likely to be formal.	
MAGAZINE ARTICLE	• Written to attract interest. • Topic may be of current interest in the media. • May start with a story of an individual. • Language may be informal and/or idiomatic. • Writer may use quotations.	• Read quickly for interest. • Understand the main point or concept.
NEWSPAPER STORY		• Read quickly for information. • May read only the first few paragraphs, then skim the rest of the story.
REPORT	• Provides information about a specific, limited topic. • Usually divided into sections: introduction, methods, results and discussion or recommendations. • Often has charts, graphs and tables. • May contain citations and references.	
ESSAY		• Read to find the thesis statement. • Read topic sentences to confirm main points. • May read paragraphs for details. • Conclusion should confirm main points from thesis.
E-MAIL	• Written for a wide variety of purposes. • Is often short. • Language may be formal or informal depending on topic, writer or recipient.	

TYPE OF TEXT	CHARACTERISTICS OF TEXT	HOW TO READ EFFICIENTLY
WEBSITE		• Skim to identify the topic/subject. • Scan for details you want to know about.
NOVEL	• Text is longer and usually narrative.	• Read for pleasure.

B. Skim Reading 3 and identify its text type. How do you know?

_____

_____

C. Skim the reading once more to identify the following key information.

1 How long is it? _____

2 Who wrote it? _____

3 When was it written? _____

4 What is the topic? _____

5 What are the main points? _____

_____

_____

_____

VOCABULARY BUILD

A. Here are some words and expressions from Reading 3. Read their definitions. Then, fill in the blanks in the sentences that follow with the best word or expression.

WORD/EXPRESSION	DEFINITION
approximately* (adv.)	close to an exact number, roughly
area* (n.)	specific place (area of a country) or field of study (area of study)
concentrated* (adj.)	present in large numbers
conversely* (conj.)	used to show opposites
domestic* (adj.)	relating to a specific, single country
fluctuated* (v.)	changed irregularly
generating* (v.)	causing, or producing
incentives* (n.)	things that encourage you to work harder
majority* of (n.)	most of the people in a group (over 50 percent)

▶

WORD/EXPRESSION	DEFINITION
on the part of (exp.)	through actions of a specific person or group of people
public administration* (n.)	field of study that prepares students to work in the federal, provincial or local governments
sector* (n.)	area of activities, especially business
significantly* (adv.)	to an important degree
source* (n.)	where you get something from (i.e., the origin)
student aid* (n.)	government financial support for students
trends* (n.)	ways in which something changes over time
visible minority* (n.)	small group of people who are easily identifiable (because of race or skin colour) within a larger group

*Appears on the Academic Word List

1 In 2008, the most popular fields of study were business, management and _____ (23 percent), architecture, engineering and related technologies (16 percent) and social and behavioural sciences and law (13 percent).

2 In November 2010, AUCC led a delegation of fifteen university presidents to India, where more than $4 million in _____ targeted to bring Indian students to Canada was announced.

3 In 2010, international students represented _____ 8 percent of full-time undergraduate students in Canada, _____ 18 percent of full-time master's students and 23 percent of full-time Ph.D. students.

4 While international students are represented in every major area of study, they are more _____ in certain areas.

5 For example, 23 percent of international students study business, management and public administration, compared to 14 percent of _____ students, and 15 percent of international students study architecture, engineering and related studies, compared to 8 percent of domestic students. _____, a greater percentage of domestic students were enrolled in social and behavioural sciences and law and the humanities.

6 Between 1980 and 1995, the number of full-time international students _____ widely.

7 Recruitment activities in France led to steady increases in students, _____ more than 7, 100 students in 2008 and overtaking the U.S. as the second leading sending country.

⑧ It is interesting to note how quickly the international student market has grown, where that growth is taking place, and also how quickly students respond to recruitment efforts and _____ put in place by their own or other countries.

⑨ In 1980, international students came to Canada from approximately 175 countries, with the _____ (52 percent) of students coming from Hong Kong, the U.S., Malaysia, the UK and Iran.

⑩ Over the last thirty years, the proportion of _____, international students and even faculty from other countries has grown _____.

⑪ There has been a concerted effort on the part of the Canadian higher education _____ to attract students from India.

⑫ Despite the growth in the number of _____ countries, almost half of all international students continued to come from one of five countries: China, France, the U.S., India and South Korea.

⑬ We compared enrolment _____ of international and domestic students by discipline.

⑭ This growth was driven in part by substantial investments _____ the Saudi government.

READING ❸   **Enrolment Trends**

A. Read the text and answer the multiple-choice questions that follow.

Enrolment of International Students in Canadian Universities

Canadian universities are becoming increasingly internationalized. Over the last thirty years, the proportion of visible minorities, international students and even faculty from other countries has grown significantly. More universities are engaging in inter-
5 national research collaborations; more international students are coming from a larger number of countries; and more Canadian students are taking advantage of international learning and research opportunities abroad.

Between 1980 and 1995, the number of full-time international students fluctuated widely. Strong increases at the beginning and end of the 1980s were followed by
10 periods of similarly strong declines so that enrolment in 1995 was almost the same as in 1980. But since 1995, international enrolment has grown rapidly. In 2010, there were 3.5 times more international students enrolled at Canadian universities

than in 1995, or 90,000 in 2010 compared to 25,500 in 1995. An additional 13,000 international students were studying part-time in 2010.

15 In 2010, international students represented approximately 8 percent of full-time undergraduate students in Canada, approximately 18 percent of full-time master's students and 23 percent of full-time Ph.D. students. Greater rep-
20 resentation of international students at the graduate level is not unique to Canada. For example, in the U.S., visa students represent about 2 percent of full-time undergraduate students in four-year public universities and about
25 23 percent of full-time graduate students. In the UK, international students represent 55 percent of the graduate student body.

Since 1995, enrolment of international students in every major field of study has grown strongly
30 in Canadian universities. The number of international students has doubled in education, and there were four-fold increases in visual and performing arts and business, management and public administration. In 2008, the most popular
35 fields of study were business, management and public administration (23 percent), architecture, engineering and related technologies (16 percent) and social and behavioural sciences and law (13 percent).

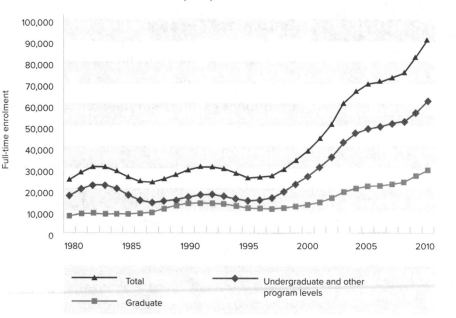

Recruitment activities have helped triple international student enrolment numbers since 1998

Source: Statistics Canada data and AUCC estimates

When we compared enrolment trends of international and domestic students by discipline, it became clear that while international students are represented in every
40 major area of study, they are more concentrated in certain areas. For example, 23 percent of international students study business, management and public admin- istration, compared to 14 percent of domestic students, and 15 percent of interna- tional students study architecture, engineering and related studies, compared to 8 percent of domestic students. Conversely, a greater percentage of domestic students
45 were enrolled in social and behavioural sciences and law and the humanities.

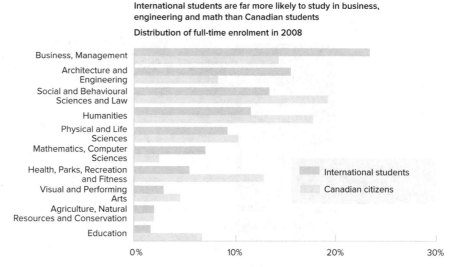

International students are far more likely to study in business, engineering and math than Canadian students

Distribution of full-time enrolment in 2008

Source: Statistics Canada

In 1980, international students came to Canada from approximately 175 countries, with the majority (52 percent) of students coming from Hong Kong, the U.S., Malaysia, the UK and Iran. By 2008, the number of source countries had increased to 200. Despite the growth in the number of source countries, almost half of all international
50 students continued to come from one of five countries: China, France, the U.S., India and South Korea. Close to 16,000 students came from China, which has been Canada's top source of international students since 2001. Recruitment activities in France led to steady increases in students, generating more than 7,100 students in 2008 and overtaking the U.S. as the second leading sending country. More than 6,600 students
55 came from the U.S.; India is in fourth place, sending approximately 2,900 students and approximately 2,780 students came to Canada from South Korea.

The next nine jurisdictions—Iran, Saudi Arabia, Hong Kong, Japan, Pakistan, Taiwan, Germany, Mexico and Nigeria—account for 16 percent of Canada's full-time interna- tional students. These nine countries sent between 1,000 and 2,200 students each
60 to Canada. The remaining countries sent fewer than 1,000 students each and accounted for one-third of international students, providing Canadian-born students with a tremendous breadth of culture in the classroom.

It is interesting to note how quickly the international student market has grown, where that growth is taking place, and also how quickly students respond to recruit-
65 ment efforts and incentives put in place by their own or other countries. For example, in 1980, there were only 650 Indian students enrolled at Canadian institutions. Indian student enrolment fluctuated between 1980 and 1997, when it began to grow rapidly. By 2008, there were almost 3,000 Indian students registered at Canadian

Top source countries have changed since 1980

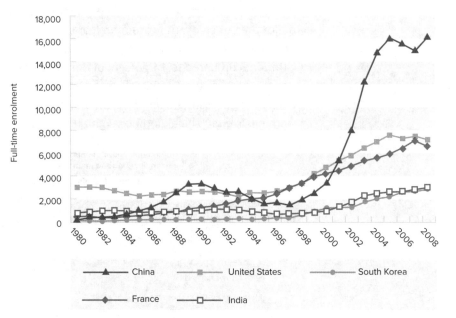

Source: Statistics Canada data and AUCC estimates

universities—an approximate five-fold increase since 1997. Enrolment of Indian
70 students is also likely to continue to grow in future years because the population in
India is growing rapidly, and because there has been a concerted effort on the part
of the Canadian higher education sector to attract students from India. For example,
in November 2010, AUCC led a delegation of fifteen university presidents to India,

where more than $4 million in student aid targeted to bring
75 Indian students to Canada was announced.[1]

In recent years, the BC-based Network Centre of Excellence
MITACS, as well as the governments of Ontario and Quebec, has
also introduced initiatives to attract students from India.

Saudi Arabia is another example of a country that is increasingly
80 sending students to Canada. In 2008–2009, Saudi Arabia became
the seventh leading source country, up from thirteenth position
the year before. This growth was driven in part by substantial
investments on the part of the Saudi government, and in part by
recruitment efforts of various Canadian institutions, working in
85 collaboration with their counterparts abroad.

… Canada is not alone in attracting more international students.
The recent growth rate of international students in Canada's universities is similar to enrolment growth in nations such as Japan,
Sweden, Norway and Finland. Countries such as the Netherlands,
90 New Zealand, Korea and the Czech Republic, which have historically attracted very small numbers of international students, are
growing at a faster pace and generating greater competition for
students, particularly from Asia and within the EU.

---

1. Many of these new scholarships were announced as part of AUCC's mission to India that took place in
   November 2010. For more information, visit www.aucc.ca.

AUCC. (2011). Trends in higher education. Volume 1, Enrolment (p. 15–18). Retrieved from: http://www.aucc.ca/
wp-content/uploads/2011/05/trends-2011-vol1-enrolment-e.pdf

B. Circle the best answer to complete the following. When you have finished, compare your answers with a classmate's.

1 International student enrolment at Canadian universities is …

a) decreasing.

b) increasing.

c) remaining constant.

2 Numbers of international students are greater at the …

a) undergraduate level.

b) graduate level.

c) faculty level.

3 Since 1995, numbers of international students have grown in …

a) all fields of study.

b) education only.

c) public administration only.

4 International students and domestic (Canadian) students are …

a) equally represented in all fields of study.

b) not equally represented in all fields of study.

5 More international students than domestic students study in the fields of … (Circle all that apply.)

a) social and behavioural sciences, law and the humanities.

b) business, management and public administration.

c) architecture, engineering and related studies.

6 Which country is the source of the majority of Canada's international students?

a) China

b) France

c) the U.S.

d) Iran

7 From which two source countries are the numbers of students expected to increase due to government incentives?

a) China and Iran

b) Germany and Mexico

c) India and Saudi Arabia

8 Which is a true statement about the international student market?

a) Canada is one of many countries competing for the brightest international students.

b) International student enrolment in Japan, Sweden, Norway and Finland is decreasing.

c) The Netherlands, New Zealand, Korea and the Czech Republic have always attracted large numbers of international students.

C. To reinforce sentence pattern information from Focus on Writing (page 36), review Reading 3 and identify one or two sentences for each of the five patterns. Write the sentences in your notebooks and label phrases, independent clauses, dependent clauses and subordinate, coordinate and adverbial adjectives.

D. In Reading 3, writers describe numerical or statistical information using a variety of words and phrases. Learning these words and phrases will help you write about statistics in this chapter's Final Assignment. In the following table, look at the parts of the sentences in bold to become aware of some of the words and phrases the writer used. Then, find two more examples in the reading for each use.

COMPARES NUMBERS	
LINE 19	**Greater representation** of international students at the graduate level **is not unique** to Canada.
LINE 40	For example, 23 percent of international students study business, management and public administration, **compared to** 14 percent of domestic students ...
LINE 44	Conversely, **a greater percentage of** domestic students were enrolled in ...

LINE_____: _____

_____

LINE_____: _____

_____

CONNECTS NUMBERS TO A TIME PERIOD	
LINE 1	**Over the last thirty years, the proportion of** visible minorities, international students and even faculty from other countries **has grown significantly**.
LINE 11	But **since 1995**, international enrolment **has grown rapidly**.
LINE 11	**In 2010, there were 3.5 times more** international students enrolled at Canadian universities **than in 1995** ...

LINE_____: _____

_____

LINE_____: _____

_____

SHOWS NUMBERS ARE INCREASING OR DECREASING	
LINE 9	**Strong increases** at the beginning and end of the 1980s ...
LINE 13	**An additional** 13,000 international students were studying part-time in 2010.
LINE 89	Countries such as the Netherlands, New Zealand, Korea and the Czech Republic ... are growing at a **faster pace** ...

LINE_____: _____

_____

LINE_____: _____

_____

E. Write sentences about the statistics in the following table to practise using some of the preceding words and phrases. When you have written five sentences, show your sentences to a classmate and work together to edit them. Share your best sentences with the class.

Example: **Over the last thirty years**, the total number of students studying at Canadian universities **has grown rapidly**.

FULL- AND PART-TIME UNDERGRADUATE STUDENTS STUDYING IN CANADA			
YEAR	FULL-TIME STUDENTS	PART-TIME STUDENTS	TOTAL STUDENTS
1980	325,000	200,000	525,000
1990	450,000	300,000	750,000
2000	575,000	200,000	775,000
2010	750,000	200,000	950,000

FINAL ASSIGNMENT
Design a Survey and Write an Extended Report

Use what you know about question format to design a survey to discover people's opinions about education. By asking your survey questions, you will generate data that you can use to write a report.

1 Choose one of the following topics for your report.
- Should colleges/universities increase tuition for international students studying in foreign countries?
- Should colleges/universities increase the number of international students?
- Should colleges/universities increase the number of domestic students?
- Should colleges/universities increase the number of students in specific academic programs?
- Should colleges/universities increase their efforts to recruit international students?

2 The people you survey are called *participants*. Create a series of questions (at least five) to discover the participants' opinions about your chosen topic. You can ask *closed* questions, *Likert scale* questions and *multiple-choice* questions.

- Closed questions are questions that have *yes* or *no* answers.

  Example: Are sports an important part of education?   Yes ☐   No ☐

- Likert scale questions ask people to rate their opinions on a scale of 1 to 5.

  Example: How important is small class size (twenty students or fewer) to a good education?
  1 very important
  2 somewhat important
  3 neither important nor unimportant
  4 unimportant
  5 completely irrelevant

- Multiple-choice questions provide possible answers for your participants.

  Example: What is the most important goal of a good education?
  a) to provide high-quality academics
  b) to develop self-esteem and confidence
  c) to develop a love of learning
  d) to promote community involvement
  e) to provide employment training

3 Once you have a set of questions, ask a classmate or the teacher to review them. Make sure you are using correct question format. Write the questions on a separate sheet of paper. Leave space to record the participants' answers.

4 Conduct your survey. Ask at least twelve participants.

5 Show your results in a table, chart or graph.

6 Write a report based on the information you gathered. Your report should include the four sections that are common in reports: introduction, method, results and discussion. Use your knowledge of sentence structure to add interest to your writing. Refer to the Models Chapter (page 179 and 181) to see examples of a survey and a report and to learn more about how to design and write one.

CHAPTER 3

Consumer Behaviour and Innovation

In the world of business, nothing is more important than knowing what the consumer will buy. Companies may spend a significant amount of time and money trying to determine how consumers behave and why they will purchase one product but not another. A business must understand this behaviour if it is to be successful.

Once a company knows consumers, it can create new products, or innovate, in order to motivate customers to buy.

In this chapter,
you will

- use new vocabulary related to consumer behaviour and innovation;

- use parallel structure to write easy-to-understand sentences;

- learn how to "read smart";

- develop an awareness of text organization in order to read more efficiently;

- write definition sentences to provide essential information to readers;

- write process essays.

GEARING UP

A. Working in a small group, discuss the answers to the following questions.

- How do you usually hear about new products?

- Do you always want to be the first to have the newest, latest, hottest product, or do you wait until others have tried it out?

- What do you consider before you buy a new product?

- When you do decide to buy a product, what influences your decision?

B. Discuss buying a new pair of shoes. List the factors that will influence your decision.

A. This reading lists a number of influences on consumer behaviour and groups them into four types. Read the text and when you have finished, fill in the first two columns of the table that follows to show the four categories and the various factors that influence consumer behaviour.

Understanding Consumer Behaviour

Market research in its many forms can be of great help to marketing managers in understanding how the common traits of a market segment affect consumers' purchasing decisions. Why do people buy DVDs? What desire are they fulfilling? Is there
5 a psychological or sociological explanation for why consumers purchase one product and not another? These questions and many others are addressed in the area of

marketing known as consumer behaviour. Consumer behaviour focuses on the decision process by which customers come to purchase and consume a
10 product or service.

Influences on Consumer Behaviour

To understand consumer behaviour, marketers draw heavily on the fields of psychology and sociology. The result is a focus on four major influences on
15 consumer behaviour: psychological, personal, social and cultural. By identifying the four influences that are most active, marketers try to explain consumer choices and predict future purchasing behaviour:

• *Psychological influences* include an individual's motivations, perceptions, ability to
20 learn and attitudes.
• *Personal influences* include lifestyle, personality, economic status and life-cycle stage.
• *Social influences* include family, opinion leaders (people whose opinions are sought by others) and reference groups such as friends, co-workers and professional associates.
• *Cultural influences* include culture (the "way of living" that distinguishes one large
25 group from another), subculture (smaller groups, such as ethnic groups, with shared values) and social class (the cultural ranking of groups according to criteria such as background, occupation and income).

Although these factors can have a strong impact on a consumer's choices, their effect on actual purchases is sometimes weak or negligible. Some consumers, for example,
30 exhibit high brand loyalty—they regularly purchase products because they are satisfied with their performance. Such people (for example, users of Craftsman tools) are less subject to influence and stick with preferred brands. On the other hand, the clothes you wear and the food you eat often reflect social and psychological influences on your consuming behaviour.

Griffin, R.W., Ebert, R.J., Starke, F.A., & Lang, M.D. (2011). Understanding marketing processes and consumer behaviour. In *Business* (7th ed., pp. 494–495). Toronto, ON: Pearson Education Canada.

TYPES OF INFLUENCE	INFLUENCES MENTIONED IN READING	INFLUENCES FROM GROUP DISCUSSION
psychological		

B. When columns one and two are complete, check your information with a class-mate. Then, return to your notes from Gearing Up and, in column three, list the influences that you discussed, classifying them according to type.

FOCUS ON WRITING

Using Parallelism in Writing

The following sentences are taken from the reading. Look at them carefully and think about what they have in common.

LINE 14: The result is a focus on four major influences on consumer behaviour: psychological, personal, social and cultural.

LINE 19: *Psychological influences* include an individual's motivations, perceptions, ability to learn and attitudes.

LINE 21: *Personal influences* include lifestyle, personality, economic status and life-cycle stage.

You may have noticed that these sentences list items. Now take a closer look at how the items are listed.

In the first sentence, each item is a one-word adjective used to describe the type of influence (psychological, personal, social, cultural), and all end in *-al*. You may also have noticed that the way this list is written creates a structure that helps the reader see the similarity of the listed items. This is called *parallelism*.

In the third sentence, each of the words in the series is a noun, which creates parallelism in the sentence. But if you look carefully, the first two items are one-word nouns and the second two are adjective + noun combinations. We can try to improve the parallel structure in the sentence by making all the items adjective + noun combinations.

Example: *Personal influences* include **lifestyle preference**, **personality type**, economic status and life-cycle stage.

The sentence now has improved parallel structure, making it easier to understand and giving it a smoother rhythm.

A. Modify the second sentence by improving the parallel structure. After the word "individual's," four items are listed. Three of them are one-word nouns. Change "ability to learn" into a one-word noun to match the others.

Psychological influences include an individual's motivations, perceptions,

_____ and attitudes.

These sentences were adapted from Reading 2, page 57.

B. Improve the following sentences by using similar grammatical forms to list items. Hints for the first four sentences are in parentheses.

❶ Failure to adjust to these differences can result in ineffective marketing or mistakes. (Match adjective-noun combinations.)

_____

_____

❷ For example, the cultural shift toward greater concern about health and fitness has created a huge industry for health-and-fitness services, exercise equipment and clothing, organic foods and a variety of diets. (Match adjective-noun combinations.)

_____

_____

_____

_____

❸ Subcultures include nationalities, religions of all kinds, groups from different races and people from different geographic regions. (Match one-word nouns.)

_____

_____

_____

❹ The shift toward informality has resulted in more demand for clothing that is more relaxed and furniture that is simple for our homes. (Find adjective-noun combinations for both items.)

_____

_____

_____

❺ An annual poll by *Maclean's Magazine* suggests that the majority of Canadians value freedom, the beauty of our natural landscape, our beliefs in respect, equality and fair treatment, our flag, our social safety net, our International role and our multicultural and multiracial makeup.

_____

_____

_____

_____

Work with other students to match the words from the reading to their meanings in the opposite column. When you have finished, check your answers with another group and confirm them as a class.

MARKETING WORDS

① Baby Boomers (n.)   _____ group that is different from the majority

② census (n.)   _____ part of something larger

③ distinct* (adj.)   _____ employment or job

④ ethnic* group (n.)   _____ living

⑤ occupation* (n.)   _____ selected group to sell to

⑥ residing* (v.)   _____ official process of counting people

⑦ segment (n.)   _____ change

⑧ shift (n.)   _____ group identified by race or nationality

⑨ target* market (n.)   _____ different or separate

⑩ visible minority (n.)   _____ people born after World War II (1946–1966)

ACADEMIC WORDS

① commodities* (n.)   _____ include some but not all of the same things

② contrary* (adj.)   _____ understand in a certain way

③ exhibit* (v.)   _____ make stronger

④ exceeds* (v.)   _____ demonstrate or show

⑤ interpret* (v.)   _____ not flexible

⑥ dominate* (v.)   _____ opposite

⑦ linked* (adj.)   _____ is greater than

⑧ overlap* (v.)   _____ form the majority of

⑨ reinforce* (v.)   _____ connected

⑩ rigid (adj.)   _____ products bought and sold

* Appears on the Academic Word List

Although you have just matched words from the reading to their meanings, there may still be words you have not yet learned. Use the strategies you read about in Chapter 1 (page 5–6):

• Guess the meaning from the context.

• Guess the meaning from root words, prefixes and suffixes.

• Keep reading without knowing the meaning of every word. Ignore the word if it is used only once or is not important to the overall meaning.

Learning to Read Smart

Generally, for most of your academic reading, you will want to read fast and remember what you read. In order to accomplish this, you should "read smart." Here are some tips that can help you read quickly, understand the main points and think critically about what you read so that you will remember the content.

Figure out exactly what you are reading.

This is important because different kinds of writing are organized in different ways. If you know how the writing is organized, you can find the main points quickly. This type of reading is called *skimming*.

- Textbooks are usually very structured. They have headings and subheadings, and the topic sentence of each paragraph clearly expresses the main point of the paragraph. Concluding sentences often restate the main points of the paragraph. Of course, you should also look at pictures and read captions.
- Magazine and newspaper articles, including Internet articles, are organized to attract attention. Generally, the main points appear in the first few paragraphs, and the details are discussed at the end of the article.
- Scholarly essays may be found in academic books, journals, magazines and newspapers and on the Internet. They are organized according to essay structure, with an introduction and thesis, body and a conclusion.

Consider what you already know about the topic.

If you are reading a textbook, looking at the table of contents can help you see how the information in one chapter relates to information that comes before and after that chapter. For other types of writing, try to remember what you already know about the topic and how it relates to the new information.

Before you begin to read, predict the information that you will learn.

What do you expect the writing to tell you? If you try to predict what you will read, you will read with greater attention.

Take short, point-form notes on each section of the reading.

The section might consist of one paragraph or several paragraphs. Use your judgment. Keep your notes short so that they are easy to review. Write in the margins. Highlight key points. Remember, however, that if you highlight too much information, it will be difficult to review quickly later on.

When you have finished the reading, use your critical thinking skills.

Write short notes about what *you think* about the content, not the content itself. For example, how important is this information? Does the information complement your prior knowledge of the topic? Is the information surprising in any way? Do you agree or disagree with the information? Is the writing biased? All of these observations can help you not only remember the information, but also decide how important it is to your academic success.

Applying Read Smart Skills

Reading 2 is a longer reading, providing you with a perfect opportunity to practise read smart skills.

A. ① What type of text are you reading?

_____

② Consider what you already know about the topic. Reading 1 (page 52), provided you with information about consumer behaviour. How will Reading 2 build on that?

_____

_____

_____

③ Before you start to read, predict the information you will learn from the reading. What do you think this reading will be about?

_____

_____

B. With another student, go through the reading and divide it into sections. As you read, write short, point-form notes on each section. Key definitions have been written in the margins as examples. You will also want to write notes on the main points in the margins.

C. After you read the text, go back to question 3. Was your prediction correct?

READING ②

Consumer purchases are influenced strongly by cultural, social, personal and psychological factors.

Characteristics Affecting Consumer Behaviour

Consumer purchases are influenced strongly by cultural, social, personal and psychological characteristics, as shown in Figure 6-2. For the most part, marketers cannot control such factors, but they must consider them.

FIGURE 6.2 Factors influencing consumer behaviour

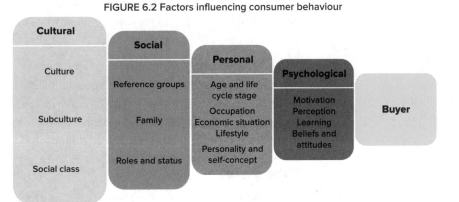

Cultural factors exert a broad and deep influence on consumer behaviour. The
5 marketer needs to understand the role played by the buyer's *culture*, *subculture* and *social class*.

Culture Characteristics Affecting Consumer Behaviour

Culture is the most basic cause of a person's wants and behaviour. Human behaviour is largely learned. Growing up in a society, a child learns basic values, perceptions,

10 wants and behaviours from the family and other important institutions. A child in the United States normally learns or is exposed to the following values: achievement
15 and success, activity and involvement, efficiency and practicality, progress, hard work, material comfort, individualism, freedom, humanitarianism, youthfulness
20 and fitness and health. In contrast, a *Maclean's Magazine* annual poll of Canadian values suggests that the majority of Canadians treasure freedom; the beauty of our natural
25 landscape; our beliefs in respect, equality and fair treatment; our flag; our social safety net; our international role; and our multicultural and multiracial [origins]. We see ourselves as unique and distinctly different from Americans. One commonality between our two cultures, however, for better or worse, is that we are
30 a consumer culture, and marketing practices reinforce this as a way of life.[1]

Every group or society has a culture, and cultural influences on buying behaviour may vary greatly from country to country. Failure to adjust to these differences can result in ineffective marketing or embarrassing mistakes. It should not be assumed, however, that culture is a homogeneous system of shared meaning, way of life or
35 unifying values.[2]

It is too broad a generalization to say, for example, that Canadians have one culture and the Japanese have another. In diverse societies, such as Canada, there is a multiplicity of overlapping cultural groupings. These in turn are influenced by the fact that we are part of a global marketplace. Marketing practices and global media
40 influence our values and consumption behaviours and even affect how we interpret and make sense of the world around us.

Marketers are always trying to spot *cultural shifts* in order to discover new products that might be wanted. For example, the cultural shift toward greater concern about health and fitness has created a huge industry for health-and-fitness services, exercise
45 equipment and clothing, organic foods and a variety of diets. The shift toward informality has resulted in more demand for casual clothing and simpler home furnishings.

Subculture

Each culture contains smaller subcultures, or groups of people with shared value systems based on common life experiences and situations. Subcultures include

---

1. Allan R. Gregg, Strains across the border, *Maclean's*, December 30, 2002, accessed at www.macleans.ca; and *Maclean's* annual poll, *Maclean's*, November 21, 2007, accessed at www.macleans.ca.
2. For a deeper discussion of consumer culture theory, see Eric J. Arnold and Craig J. Thompson, Consumer culture theory (CCT): Twenty years of research, *Journal of Consumer Research, 31* (4), 2005, pp. 868–883.

50 nationalities, religions, racial groups and geographic regions. Many subcultures make up important market segments, and marketers often design products and marketing programs tailored to their needs. Examples of four such important subculture groups in Canada include regional subcultures, founding nat-

55 ions, ethnic subcultures and mature consumers.

Canada is a regional country, so marketers may develop distinctive programs for the

60 Atlantic Provinces, Quebec, Central Canada, the Prairies and British Columbia. The sheer size of the country and its varied geographic features

65 and climate has certainly shaped regional character and personality. For example, Atlantic Canada is largely defined by its proximity to

70 and historical relationship with the sea. Equally, the isolation imposed by the mountain barrier, along with the abundance and grandeur of British Columbia's natural environment, shaped the outlook of that region's residents. Immigration has also had a differential effect on the different regions within Canada. The economy of each region furthers these differences. The fate of regions linked to the rise and fall of

75 commodities, such as fish, timber, wheat, minerals or oil, has affected regional mindsets as well as economies. Perceived disparities in political power have also increased regionalism, especially in Quebec, Newfoundland and Labrador and Alberta.[3]

Canada had three founding nations: the English, French and Aboriginal peoples. The unique history and language of each of these nations has driven many of the cultural

80 differences that result in different buying behaviours across Canada. The most recent census results (2006) reported that people noting their English-language roots (Anglophones) accounted for approximately 57 percent of the population, people whose mother tongue is French (Francophones) made up approximately 22 percent of the population, and those reporting Aboriginal ancestry represented 3.7 percent of the

85 total population.

According to Statistics Canada, roughly one out of every five people in Canada could be a member of a visible minority by 2017, when Canada celebrates its 150th anniversary. Two hundred thousand new immigrants come to Canada each year.[4]

Thus, being sensitive to their cultural values is important, because 70 percent of the

90 visible minority population were born outside Canada. According to Balmoral Marketing, an ethnic ad agency in Toronto, many firms are now spending as much as 15 percent of their total communications budget on ethnic marketing.[5]

3. The Centre for Canadian Studies, 2001, *The political voice of Canadian regional identities*, at http://culturescope.ca/even.php?ID=9417201&ID2=DO_TOPIC, accessed September 2006.
4. Statistics Canada, Study: Canada's visible minority population in 2017, *The Daily*, March 22, 2005.
5. Hamlin Grange and Don Miller, How to leverage diversity, *Marketing Magazine*, August 29, 2005.

People with Chinese background are still the largest group among visible minorities in Canada. According to a 2006 *Marketing Magazine* report, 3.74 percent of Canada's
95 population is Chinese, with 40 percent of this group residing in Toronto and 31 percent living in Vancouver. The average Chinese household spends $63,500 each year, slightly higher than the Canadian average of $58,500. People of South Asian origin

(currently 23 percent of visible minorities) may represent as large a marketplace by
100 2017. According to a recent survey, 50 percent of South Asians say their opinion of a company would improve if they saw the ads on South Asian TV, and 62 percent stated that they would look more positively on com-
105 panies that sponsored community events.

Canadian companies are realizing the importance of culturally relevant advertising that includes a multimedia approach to reach the Chinese Canadian market. A 2008 poll, con-
110 ducted by Solutions Research Group, revealed that Internet use among Chinese Canadians exceeds time spent listening to radio and watching TV combined. Internet portals such as Toronto-based 51.ca or Ottawa-based comefromchina.com, which serve as free
115 markets for information for Canada's Chinese community, have captured the attention of many Canadian advertisers. Chinese Canadians appreciate advertising delivered in their native tongue. "There's a certain emotional connection a person makes when somebody speaks their own language," said Solutions Research Group president Kaan Yigit. ["It shows respect and makes you feel like you're
120 being acknowledged."][6]

Though age is a demographic variable, some researchers also contend that different age cohorts have distinct cultures. As of July 2008, the median age in Canada was 39.4 years and higher than ever before (median age is defined as the point where exactly half of the population is older, and the other half is younger). According to
125 the 2001 census, the median age was 37.6. To see how rapidly the Canadian population has aged, it is interesting to note that the median age in Canada in 1966 (the year when the last of the Baby Boomers were born) was 25.4 years. Thus, [older individuals dominate Canada's working-age population today although] there are regional variations. Newfoundland and Labrador has the oldest population with a
130 median age of 42.5. Alberta is the youngest, with a median age of 35.7. Because of high immigration rates, however, Canada's population is not aging as fast as the population of the United States.

As the Canadian population ages, mature consumers are becoming a very attractive market. By 2015, the entire Baby Boom generation, the largest and wealthiest
135 demographic cohort in the country for more than half a century, will have moved into the fifty-plus age bracket. They will control a larger proportion of wealth, income and consumption than any current or previous generation. Despite some financial

6. Huixia Sun, Chinese websites beat economic blues, *The Vancouver Sun*, May 15, 2009; and Chris Powell, New Chinese Canadians prefer Internet to TV: Diversity study, *Marketing Magazine*, April 2008.

setbacks resulting from the recent economic crisis, mature consumers remain an attractive market for companies in all industries, from pharmaceuticals, groceries, beauty products and clothing to consumer electronics, travel and entertainment and financial services.[7]

Contrary to popular belief, mature consumers are not "stuck in their ways." On the contrary, a recent American Association of Retired Persons study showed that older consumers for products such as stereos, computers and mobile phones are more willing to shop around and switch brands than their younger Generation-X counterparts. For example, notes one expert, "Some 25 percent of Apple's iPhones—the epitome of cool, cutting-edge product—have been bought by people over fifty.[8]

The growing [segment] of mature consumers creates an attractive market for convenient services. For example, Home Depot and Lowe's now target older consumers who are less enthusiastic about do-it-yourself chores than with "do-it-for-me" handyman services. And their desire to look as young as they feel also makes more-mature consumers good candidates for cosmetics and personal care products, health foods, fitness products and other items that combat the effects of aging. The best strategy is to appeal to their active multi-dimensional lives. For example, Dove's pro-age hair and skin care product line claims that "Beauty has no age limit." Pro-age ads feature active and attractive, real women who seem to be benefitting from the product's promise. Says one ad, "Dove created pro-age to reflect the unique needs of women in their best years. This isn't anti-age, it's pro-age."[9]

Social Class

Social Classes
Relatively permanent and ordered divisions in a society whose members share similar values, interests and behaviours

Almost every society has some form of social class structure. Social classes are society's relatively permanent and ordered divisions whose members share similar values, interests and behaviours. Social class is not determined by a single factor, such as income, but is measured as a combination of occupation, income, education, wealth and other variables. In some social systems, members of different classes … cannot change their social positions. In North America, however, the lines between social classes are not fixed and rigid; people can move to a higher social class or drop into a lower one.

Most Canadians see themselves as middle class, and we are less likely willing to think of ourselves in terms of social class than our neighbours south of the border. It is for this reason that the New Democratic Party no longer tries to appeal to "the working class" but to "ordinary Canadians." Marketers are interested in social class because people within a given social class tend to exhibit similar buying behaviour. Social classes show distinct product and brand preferences in areas such as clothing, home furnishings, leisure activity and automobiles.

Citations and Footnotes
In Chapter 1, you worked with in-text citations and a reference section at the end of the readings. In this chapter, the authors are using a different system of documenting their original sources. Both are correct, and you will learn more about referencing in Chapter 5.

---

7. See Noreen O'Leary, Squeeze play, *Adweek*, January 12, 2009, pp. 8–9; and Emily Brandon, Planning to retire: 10 things you didn't know about Baby Boomers, USNews.com, January 15, 2009, accessed at www.usnews.com.
8. Boom time of America's new retirees feel entitled to relax and intend to spend, *Financial Times*, December 6, 2007, p. 9.
9. See www.dove.us/#/products/collections/proage.aspx, accessed November 2009.

Armstrong, G., Kotler, P., Trifts, V., Buchwitz, L. & Finlayson, P. (2012). Understanding consumer and business buyer behaviour. In *Marketing: An introduction* (4th Canadian ed., pp. 205–209). Toronto, ON: Pearson Education Canada.

Use your margin notes to answer the following questions. If you have written good margin notes, you may not have to reread the text.

1 Which factors influence consumer behaviour?

_____

_____

2 What is culture?

_____

_____

3 Why is it important for marketers to be aware of cultural shifts?

_____

_____

4 What is subculture? Give an example.

_____

_____

5 This reading gives a lot of detailed information about Canadian subcultures. Which subcultures are discussed in this reading?

_____

_____

_____

6 What are the unique characteristics of the Chinese subculture in Canada that marketers should be aware of?

_____

_____

_____

7 What is the age group in Canada that marketers are increasingly trying to reach? Why? Give an example.

_____

_____

_____

8 What are social classes?

_____

_____

9 What view of social class do most Canadians have? Why is this important?

_____

_____

_____

WARM-UP ASSIGNMENT

Write a Short Process Essay

Write a short process essay to explain how cultural factors might influence the consumer behaviour of one of the following consumers.

- Fifteen-year-old Samuel Parker has been saving his paper route money for six months to buy a pair of the coolest basketball shoes. Samuel lives in Toronto.

- Twenty-three-year-old Mary Wood is an English Second Language teacher living in an apartment in Vancouver. She wants to buy a computer.

- Nineteen-year-old Xiaoshan Wu is an engineering student in Ottawa. She lives far away from the university campus and wants to buy a car.

A process essay is written to explain how something is done—the steps or stages of a process. Refer to the Models Chapter (page 183) to see an example of a process essay and to learn more about how to write one.

Use parallel structure in your thesis and concluding statements, and in any other sentences that list items.

When you receive feedback from your teacher or your classmates on this Warm-Up Assignment, you will have some information that you can use to improve your writing on the Final Assignment.

VOCABULARY BUILD

Consider the difference between everyday language and academic language. Choose the best academic word to replace the everyday vocabulary in parentheses in the sentences below. The first one has been done for you.

ACADEMIC WORDS

adopt (v.)	compatible* (adj.)	laggard (n.)	seek* (v.)
affect* (v.)	hurdle (n.)	perceive* (v.)	venturesome (adj.)
approach* (v.)	initial* (adj.)	recession (n.)	
awareness* (n.)	innovation* (n.)	refrain from (v.)	

* Appears on the Academic Word List

1. We now look at how buyers (deal with) _____approach_____ the purchase of new products.

2. Successful companies encourage (new methods) _____ to maintain their competitive advantage.

3. Consumers (search for) _____ information about the new product.

4. To help buyers overcome this (problem) _____, Hyundai created a new marketing program.

5 For every new purchase, consumers must also consider the (start up) _____ costs and ongoing costs.

6 Consumers must make decisions about whether to (buy and use) _____ the new product.

7 Innovators, or people who buy a new product early, are often (risk takers) _____.

8 (Those people who are slow to try new products) _____ do not purchase until the product is almost a tradition.

9 The characteristics of a new product (influence) _____ its rate of adoption.

10 The early HDTVs were not (capable of being used in combination) _____ with the current broadcasting systems or programs.

11 A new product is a goods, service or idea that some customers (think of) _____ as new.

12 When consumers are worried about losing their jobs, they (stop) _____ buying expensive products.

13 Marketers must be creative to sell their products during a (economic hard times) _____.

14 A marketer's job is to encourage an (knowledge and understanding) _____ of the product he or she wants to sell.

READING ❸ — To Buy or Not to Buy

A. As a class, brainstorm new products that have come on the market in the last five years. These will likely include new technologies, but also consider services such as online grocery purchasing or online newspaper subscriptions.

Try to come up with at least ten new products or services. Write these in the first column of the following table. Then, next to each product or service, indicate whether you are aware of it, are interested in buying it (but have not bought it) or have bought it for yourself or for someone else.

B. For each product or service you list, give a reason for your choice—or refusal—to buy the product.

NEW PRODUCT OR SERVICE	AWARE OF	INTERESTED IN	HAVE BOUGHT	REASON

C. Answer the following questions about Reading 3 to practise the read smart skills you learned about on page 56.

1 Identify what kind of text it is. _____

2 The subheadings divide the reading into how many sections? _____

3 What is the purpose of the first section?

_____

4 What is the purpose of the remaining sections?

_____

5 What type of text do sections two to four remind you of?

_____

D. Read the following questions. Then, scan the text to find the answers.

1 What are the stages in the adoption process that consumers move through when they buy a new product?

_____

_____

2 What are the five groups that marketers have defined to explain why some people buy new products before others?

_____

_____

_____

3 What are the five characteristics of a new product that affect its rate of adoption (how quickly consumers are willing to buy it)?

_____

_____

_____

The Buyer Decision Process for New Products

New product
A goods, service or idea that
is perceived by some potential
customers as new

We now look at how buyers approach the purchase of new products. A new product is a goods, service or idea that is perceived by some potential customers as new. It may have been around for a while, but our interest is in how consumers learn
5 about products for the first time and make decisions on whether to adopt them. We define the adoption process as "the mental process through which an individual passes from first learning about an innovation to final adoption," and adoption as the decision by an individual to become a regular user of the product.

Stages in the Adoption Process

Adoption process
The mental process through which
an individual passes from first
hearing about an innovation to
final adoption

10 Consumers go through five stages in the process of adopting a new product.

- Awareness: The consumer becomes aware of the new product, but lacks information about it.
- Interest: The consumer seeks information about the new product.
- Evaluation: The consumer considers whether trying the new product makes sense.
15 • Trial: The consumer tries the new product on a small scale to improve his or her estimate of its value.
- Adoption: The consumer decides to make full and regular use of the new product.

This model suggests that the new-product marketer should think about how to help consumers
20 move through these stages. For example, as the recent recession set in, Hyundai discovered many potential customers were interested in buying new cars but refrained from doing so because of the uncertain economy. To help
25 buyers pass this hurdle, the carmaker offered the Hyundai Assurance Program, promising to let buyers who financed or leased a new Hyundai to return their vehicles at no cost and with no harm to their credit rating if they lost their jobs
30 or incomes within a year. Sales of the Hyundai Sonata [increased] 85 percent in the month following the start of the campaign. Other carmakers soon followed with their own assurance plans.[1]

Individual Differences in Innovativeness

People differ greatly in their readiness to try new products. In each product area,
35 there are "consumption pioneers" and early adopters. Other individuals adopt new products much later. People can be classified into the adopter categories shown in Figure 6.5. After a slow start, an increasing number of people adopt the new product. The number of adopters reaches a peak and then drops off as fewer non-adopters remain. Innovators are defined as the first 2.5 percent of the buyers to adopt a new
40 idea (those beyond two standard deviations from mean adoption time); the early adopters are the next 13.5 percent (between one and two standard deviations); and so forth.

---

1. Nick Bunkley, Hyundai, using a safety net, wins market share, *New York Times*, February 5, 2009; and Chris Woodyard and Bruce Horvitz, GM, Ford are latest offering help to those hit by job loss, *USA Today*, April 1, 2009, accessed at www.usatoday.com/money/advertising/2009-03-30-consumers-retail-job-loss_N.htm.

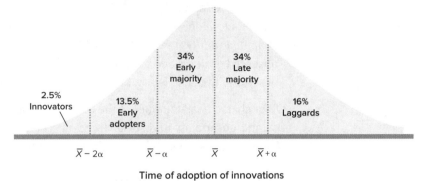

FIGURE 6.5 Adopter categorization on the basis of relative time of adoption of innovations

Time of adoption of innovations

Source: Reprinted with permission of the Free Press, a division of Simon & Schuster, from *Diffusion of innovations*, Fifth Edition, by Everett M. Rogers Copyright © 2003 by the Free Press.

The five adopter groups have differing values. *Innovators* are venturesome—they try new ideas at some risk. *Early adopters* are guided by respect—they are opinion leaders in
45 their communities and adopt new ideas early but carefully. The *early majority* are deliberate—although they rarely are leaders, they adopt new ideas before the average person. The *late majority* are skeptical—they adopt an innovation only after a majority of people have tried it. Finally, *laggards* are tradition bound—they are suspicious of changes and adopt the innovation only when it has become something of a tradition itself.

50 This adopter classification suggests that an innovating firm should research the characteristics of innovators and early adopters in their product categories and should direct marketing efforts towards them.

Influence of Product Characteristics on Rate of Adoption

The characteristics of the new product affect its rate of adoption. Some products
55 [become popular] almost overnight—for example, the iPod and iPhone, both of which flew off retailers' shelves at an astounding rate from the day they were introduced. Others take a longer time to gain acceptance. For example, the first HDTVs were introduced in North America in the 1990s, but by 2009 only about 25 percent of TV households owned a high-definition set.[2]

60 Five characteristics are especially important in influencing an innovation's rate of adoption. For example, consider the characteristics of HDTV in relation to the rate of adoption:
• *Relative advantage*: the degree to which the innovation appears superior to existing products. HDTV offers substantially improved picture quality. This [increased] its
65 rate of adoption.
• *Compatibility*: the degree to which the innovation fits the values and experiences of potential consumers. HDTV, for example, is highly compatible with the lifestyles of the TV-watching public. However, in the early years, HDTV was not yet compatible with programming and broadcasting systems, slowing adoption. Now, as more
70 and more high-definition programs and channels have become available, the rate of HDTV adoption has increased. In fact, the number of HDTV-owning households has more than doubled in just the past two years.
• *Complexity*: the degree to which the innovation is difficult to understand or use. HDTVs are not very complex. Therefore, as more programming has become avail-
75 able and prices have fallen, the rate of HDTV adoption is increasing faster than that of more complex innovations.

---

2. See U.S. HDTV penetration nears 25%, *Nielsen Wire*, December 11, 2008.

- *Divisibility*: the degree to which the innovation may be tried on a limited basis. Early HDTVs and HD cable and satellite systems were very expensive, slowing the rate of adoption. As prices fall, adoption rates are increasing.

80 • *Communicability*: the degree to which the results of using the innovation can be observed or described to others. Because HDTV lends itself to demonstration and description, its use will spread faster among consumers.

Other characteristics influence the rate of adoption, such as initial and ongoing costs, risk and uncertainty and social approval. The new-product marketer must research 85 all these factors when developing the new product and its marketing program.

Armstrong, G., Kotler, P., Trifts, V., Buchwitz, L. & Finlayson, P. (2012). Understanding consumer and business buyer behaviour. In *Marketing: An introduction* (4th Canadian ed., pp. 222–224). Toronto, ON: Pearson Education Canada.

FOCUS ON WRITING

Writing Definitions

Below are four sentences from Readings 2 and 3 that give definitions. Writing definitions is often required in academic writing. For this reason, it is useful to recognize typical sentence patterns that writers use.

A. Look at the following sentences and identify the shared characteristics and sentence structure. Some of the features are in bold to make them more obvious.

1 **Culture is** the set of basic values, perceptions, wants and behaviours **that are** learned by a member of society from family and other important institutions.

2 **Subculture is** a group of people with shared value systems **that are** based on common life experiences and situations.

3 **Social classes are** the relatively permanent and ordered divisions in a society **whose members share** similar values, interests and behaviours.

4 **A new product is** a goods, service or idea **that is** perceived by some potential customers as new.

B. In the following table, the first sentence has been rewritten to show the common sentence structure for definition sentences. Follow the same pattern and rewrite sentences two, three and four.

	WORD TO BE DEFINED	TO BE (IS/ARE)	NOUN OR NOUN PHRASE	RELATIVE PRONOUN	RELATIVE CLAUSE
1	Culture	is	the set of basic values, perceptions, wants and behaviours	that	are learned by a member of society from family and other important institutions.
2					
3					
4					

C. Working with a partner, write definition sentences for the following words from Reading 3. When you have finished, write your best sentence on the board.

❶ An **innovator** is _____

_____

_____

❷ Early **adopters** are _____

_____

_____

❸ The **early majority** is _____

_____

_____

❹ **Laggards** are _____

_____

_____

FINAL ASSIGNMENT
Write a Longer Process Essay

Return to the list of new products that you developed with your classmates in Reading 3, A (page 65). Choose one from this list as your topic for the longer process essay that you will now write.

Select a group of people you would like to write about. Define this group as a market segment by stating their age range, gender and cultural influences (culture, subculture, social class). Write a process essay to explain how a company could best market the new product to the selected market segment.

In your essay:

• Use vocabulary from the reading to refer to the stages of adoption and the individual differences in responding to new products.

• Write about the characteristics of the product that will influence (or are influencing) its rate of adoption.

• Write at least one definition sentence and use parallel structure in your thesis and concluding statements, and in any other sentences that list items.

Refer to the Models Chapter (page 183) to see an example of a process essay and to learn more about how to write one.

CHAPTER 4

Branding: The Positive and the Negative

Just about every product we buy—from clothing to computers to food—has a brand. A brand is the idea or image or any other feature that distinguishes one company's product or service from that of another company.

Companies certainly benefit from creating a brand, but what about consumers? Do they benefit from branding? Some critics argue that the answer is no. In fact, they believe that brand marketing negatively influences many people in a wide variety of ways.

In this chapter, you will

- use new vocabulary related to the positive and negative impacts of branding;
- use collocations to increase your writing fluency;
- learn strategies to become an independent language learner;
- develop an awareness of text organization to help you read more efficiently;
- write persuasive essays.

GEARING UP

A. Are there certain brands that you are familiar with and tend to buy? With a small group of students, discuss the following products. Then for each product, list those brand names that are the most popular among your group.

PRODUCT	BRAND NAME
CARS	
CELLPHONES	
CLOTHING	
COMPUTERS	
DRINKS	
FAST FOOD	
SHOES	

B. Which of the brand names that you listed do you ...

1. not know? _____
2. know about, but don't buy? _____
3. buy when possible? _____
4. absolutely have to have? _____

Brand Loyalty and Brand Equity

A. Skim Reading 1 to answer the following questions. When you have finished, compare your answers with those of a classmate. Fill in any gaps that you might have.

❶ What is brand loyalty?

_____

_____

❷ What are the three stages of brand loyalty?

_____

_____

❸ Why is it important to keep a customer loyal?

_____

_____

❹ What is brand equity, from both the consumer and corporate perspectives?

_____

_____

B. Return to Gearing Up and identify the stage of brand loyalty you have for each brand name.

_____

_____

_____

Brand Loyalty and Brand Equity

Brand loyalty is defined as the degree of consumer attachment to a particular brand of product or service. This degree of attachment can be weak or strong and varies from one product category to another. Brand loyalty is measured in three stages:
5 brand recognition, brand preference and brand insistence.[1]

Refer to the following for an illustration of these stages.

Brand recognition	Brand preference	Brand insistence
Consumer is aware of the name, benefit and package.	Brand is top-of-mind and considered a good alternative. Consumer will buy if available.	Consumer buys one brand only. If brand is not available, the purchase is postponed.

In the early stages of a product's life, the marketing objective is to create **brand recognition**, which is customer awareness of the brand name, package and/or design. Media advertising plays a key role in creating awareness. Once awareness is achieved,
10 a brand may offer customers free samples or coupons to tempt them to make the first (trial) purchase.

---

1. Dale Beckman et al. (1988). *Foundations of marketing* (pp. 316–317). Toronto, ON: Holt, Rinehart and Winston.

In the **brand preference** stage of a product's life, the brand [is an] acceptable alternative and will be purchased if it is available when needed. If it is unavailable, the consumer will switch to an equal, competitive alternative. For example, if Pepsi-Cola is requested at McDonald's and the order cannot be filled because the product is unavailable there, the consumer will usually accept the substitute, in this case Coca-Cola.

At the **brand insistence** stage, a consumer will search the market extensively for the brand he or she wants. No alternatives are acceptable, and if the brand is unavailable, the consumer is likely to postpone purchase until it is. Such a situation is a marketer's dream, a dream rarely achieved. Some critics insist that the original Coca-Cola product reached a level beyond brand insistence. So strong was the attachment that the product could not be changed. When it was changed (to New Coke), the backlash from the consumers was so strong that the company had no alternative but to bring the original product back under the name Coca-Cola Classic.

…

The task of the marketer is to keep customers loyal. Study after study has shown that it is many times more difficult and expensive to convert a new customer than it is to retain a current customer. In preserving loyalty, companies cannot take their customers for granted. Many brands are instituting customer relationship management (CRM) programs that are specifically designed to keep a customer as a customer.

…

The benefits of brands and the various levels of brand loyalty are what marketers refer to as brand equity. Brand equity is defined as the value a consumer derives from a product over and above the value derived from the physical attributes. Equity is the result of good marketing, and it is measured in terms of four variables: name awareness, a loyal customer base, perceived quality and the brand's association with a certain attribute. When Canadian brands are ranked on these criteria some familiar names pop up. The top six brands in 2010 were Thomson Reuters, TD (Toronto Dominion Bank), RBC (Royal Bank of Canada), BlackBerry, Shoppers Drug Mart and Tim Hortons.[2]

Another explanation of brand equity is directly related to monetary value. Brand equity is defined as the value of a brand to its owners as a corporate asset.[3]… On a global scale the undisputed brand equity leader in terms of value is Google. Google is valued at $86.1 billion. Other big equity brands include General Electric (GE) at $71.4 billion, Microsoft at $70.9 billion, Coca-Cola at $58.2 billion and Chinese Mobile at $57.2 billion.[4]

2. Interbrand. (2010). Best Canadian brands 2010: The definitive guide to Canada's most valuable brands. Retrieved from: http://www.interbrand.com/Libraries/Branding_Studies/Best_Canadian_Brands_2010.sflb.ashx
3. A dictionary of branding terms. See: www.landor.com
4. Matt Semansky. BlackBerry jumps up global brand rankings. *Marketing Daily*, April 21, 2008. See: www. marketingmag.ca

Tuckwell, K. (2010). Product strategy. In *Canadian marketing in action* (8th ed., pp. 217–220). Toronto, ON: Pearson Canada.

Learning Collocations

You can increase your reading and writing fluency by learning pairs or small groups of words at the same time. These groups of words are called *colloca-tions*. Collocations often appear together in recognized mini-expressions. When you know how words collocate, you know how they are used together. Research indicates that collocations represent a significant amount of all language use. Therefore, when you learn a new word, you should learn not only the meaning of the word but also how it collocates with others. Then you will know both what a word means and how to use it.

In the previous reading, there were a number of collocations with the word *brand*. In most cases, *brand* is used as an adjective that modifies a noun, as in *brand name*.

Look at Reading 1 again, more closely, and list all the collocations related to the word *brand*.

brand name _____

_____ _____

_____ _____

The following are words you saw in the last reading or will see in the next reading. Each word appears in two sentences: first in a marketing context and then, in a non-marketing context. Determine the common meaning and write a short definition (including the part of speech) for each word.

❶ slogan	a) In most advertising, a close relationship exists between a brand (such as Nike) and its **slogan** ("Just Do It").
	b) In some countries, young people risk their lives by writing anti-government **slogans** on public buildings.
DEFINITION	short phrase that is easy to remember and used by advertisers, politicians and organizations (noun)
❷ stabilize*	a) Consumer loyalty **stabilizes** market share and creates efficiency in production.
	b) The patient has been very ill, but the new medicine has **stabilized** his condition.
DEFINITION	

❸ attributes*	a) The **attributes** of innovation and intelligence are associated with the Apple brand.	
	b) She had many **attributes** of a strong leader: optimism, management skills, vision and an outgoing nature.	
DEFINITION	_____	
	_____	
❹ strategic*	a) Marketing managers must make **strategic** decisions about when and where to advertise their brands.	
	b) Gibraltar is in a **strategic** location at the mouth of the Mediterranean Sea.	
DEFINITION	_____	
	_____	
❺ perception	a) Some critics suggest that the market **perception** of a brand attribute is more important than real brand attributes.	
	b) There is widespread public **perception** that old governments should be replaced.	
DEFINITION	_____	
	_____	
❻ proposal	a) A company with a new product may ask a marketing firm for a **proposal** to create a branding strategy for the new product.	
	b) The student committee presented a **proposal** to reduce pollution at the university.	
DEFINITION	_____	
	_____	
❼ stalled	a) Exxon was going to use the name Enco but decided against it when a Japanese client told the company *enco* means "**stalled** engine" in Japanese.	
	b) Her career has **stalled**; however, his career has really progressed.	
DEFINITION	_____	
	_____	
❽ infringe	a) A brand name must not **infringe** on a name another company has already claimed.	
	b) Photocopying a chapter from a textbook **infringes** on copyright laws.	
DEFINITION	_____	
	_____	

▶

9 quirky	a) Brand names like Yahoo and Google are **quirky**.
	b) She has a **quirky** sense of humour.
DEFINITION	_____ _____
10 intuitive	a) Some brands, like the educational software brand Black-board, make **intuitive** sense.
	b) He had an **intuitive** ability to understand what his teammates needed to work best.
DEFINITION	_____ _____
11 synonymous	a) The word *google* instantly became **synonymous** with "Internet search."
	b) Learning correct grammar is not **synonymous** with using grammar correctly.
DEFINITION	_____ _____
12 resurrect	a) A company may decide to **resurrect** an old brand name if they think the public will respond to it.
	b) *Indiana Jones and the Kingdom of the Crystal Skull* was the final Indiana Jones movie, but it did not **resurrect** the series.
DEFINITION	_____ _____
13 generic	a) A **generic** or "store" brand is usually cheaper than a branded product.
	b) *Arts* is a **generic** term that includes subjects such as languages, psychology, sociology, history and geography.
DEFINITION	_____ _____
14 tangible	a) Brands such as Godiva (chocolate), Starbucks, Apple and Victoria's Secret rely less on a product's **tangible** attributes and more on creating surprise, passion and excitement around a brand.
	b) The judge had no **tangible** evidence that the man was guilty.
DEFINITION	_____ _____

▶

⑮ mission	a) When positioning a brand, the marketer should establish a **mission** for the brand and a vision for what the brand must be and do.
	b) The scientists' **mission** was no less than to find a cure for cancer.
DEFINITION	_____
	_____

* Appears on the Academic Word List

Applying Read Smart Skills

To prepare for Reading 2, review read smart skills from Chapter 3 (page 56).
- Figure out exactly what you are reading.
- Consider what you already know about the topic.
- Before you start to read, predict the information that you will learn from the reading.
- Skim the reading and try to divide it into sections. The sections may be clearly indicated by headings and subheadings, or you may have to define the sections for yourself.
- Take short, point-form notes on each section. Write in the margins.
- When you have finished the reading, use your critical thinking skills. Is your prediction correct? How important will this information be to your Final Assignment?
- Compare your notes with a classmate's. Are there any differences in your margin notes? If so, why?

READING ❷ Branding Strategy

Marketing managers responsible for brands must make high-level strategic decisions that govern the management of the brand and that guide the public and market perceptions about the brand. The main branding strategy decisions are brand name selection and brand positioning.

5 **Brand Name Selection**

A good name can add greatly to a product's success. However, finding the best brand name is a difficult task. It begins with a careful review of the product and its benefit, the target market and proposed marketing strategies. After that, naming a brand becomes part science, part art and a measure of instinct. Here [is] what brand experts
10 say are the things to consider when coming up with a new brand name:
- It should suggest something about the type of products it will brand, such as Beauty-rest, Craftsman and Snuggle.
- It should be distinctive, such as Google, Lexus and BlackBerry.
- It should be extendable, that is, not tied too closely to one product. Good names
15 that illustrate this example are Oracle, Amazon.com and Nike.

- It should be pronounceable in many languages, such as Kodak. Before changing its name to Exxon, Standard Oil of New Jersey rejected the name Enco, which it learned meant a stalled engine in Japanese.
20 - It should be capable of registration and protection as a trademark. A brand name cannot be registered if it infringes on existing brand names. Unique, "made-up" names work best for this, such as Yahoo!, Novartis and Ugg.

Choosing a new brand name is hard work. After a decade of choosing quirky names (Yahoo!, Google) or trademark-proof made-up names (Novartis, Aventis, Lycos), today's style is to
25 build brands around names that have real meaning. For example, names such as Silk (soya milk), Method (home products), Smartwater (beverages) and Blackboard (school software) are simple and make intuitive sense. But with trademark applications soaring, available new names can be hard to
30 find. Try it yourself. Pick a product and see whether you can come up with a better name for it. How about Moonshot? Tickle? Vanilla? Treehugger? Simplicity? Do a quick online search and you'll find that they are already taken.

A great brand absolutely requires a good, strong, memorable name. When Google
35 burst onto the scene in 1998, no one had to say the name twice. It was instantly memorable and, only a few short years later, it had become synonymous with "Internet search." Perhaps the greatest example of how to choose a great brand name is the story of Kodak. The name was invented after researchers discovered that the "K" sound signals strength … in many popular languages.

40 Sometimes companies resurrect brand names from the past and give them a new life. Ford sold more than seven million cars branded with the name Taurus but discontinued the brand in 2006. It didn't exactly stop making the car; it just changed the name to Ford Five Hundred. Even though it was essentially the same car, the Five Hundred flopped because the name had no meaning to consumers. Consumer
45 research conducted by Ford revealed that only 25 percent of people were aware of the Ford Five Hundred, but 80 percent of people recognized the name Taurus—in fact, it was the third strongest of all Ford's brand names (after F-150 and Mustang). So the company decided to switch the car's name back to Taurus.[1]

Once chosen, the brand name must be protected. Many firms try to build a brand
50 name that will eventually become identified with the product category. Brand names such as Kleenex, Levi's, JELL-O, BAND-AID, Scotch Tape, Formica and Ziploc have succeeded in this way. However, their very success may threaten the company's rights to the name. Many originally protected brand names—such as cellophane, aspirin, nylon, kerosene, linoleum, yo-yo, trampoline, escalator, thermos and
55 shredded wheat—are now generic words that any seller can use. To protect their brands, marketers present them by carefully using the word "brand" and the registered trademark symbol, as in "BAND-AID™ Brand Adhesive Bandages." Even the long-standing "I am stuck on BAND-AID and BAND-AID's stuck on me" jingle has now become, "I am stuck on BAND-AID brand and BAND-AID's stuck on me."

---

1. Jean Halliday, Ford resurrects Taurus name, *Advertising Age*, February 7, 2007, accessed at adage.com

60 Brand Positioning

Marketers need to position their brands clearly in target customers' minds. They can position brands at any of three levels.[2] At the lowest level, they can position the brand on product attributes. For example, Proctor and Gamble (P&G) invented the disposable diaper category with its Pampers brand. Early Pampers marketing focused on attributes such as fluid absorption, fit and disposability. In general, however, attributes are the least desirable level for brand positioning. Competitors can easily copy attributes. More importantly, customers are not interested in attributes as such; they are interested in what the attribute will do for them.

A brand can be better positioned by associating its name with a desirable benefit. Thus, Pampers can go beyond technical product attributes and talk about the resulting containment and skin-health benefits from dryness. "There are fewer wet bottoms in the world because of us," says Jim Stengel, P&G's former global marketing officer. Some successful brands positioned on benefits are Volvo (safety), FedEx (guaranteed on-time delivery), Nike (performance) and Lexus (quality).

The strongest brands go beyond attribute or benefit positioning. They are positioned on strong beliefs and values. These brands [have] an emotional [dimension]. Brands such as Godiva, Starbucks, Apple and Victoria's Secret rely less on a product's tangible attributes and more on creating surprise, passion and excitement surrounding a brand. Successful brands engage customers on a deep, emotional level. Thus, P&G knows that, to parents, Pampers mean much more than just containment and dryness. According to Stengel,

> If you go back, we often thought of P&G's brands in terms of functional benefits. But when we began listening very closely to customers, they told us Pampers meant much more to them—Pampers are more about parent-child relationships and total baby care. So we started to say, "We want to be a brand experience; we want to be there to help support parents and babies as they grow and develop."[3]

When positioning a brand, the marketer should establish a mission for the brand and a vision for what the brand must be and do. A brand is the company's promise to deliver a specific set of features, benefits, services and experiences consistently to the buyers. The brand promise must be simple and honest. Motel 6, for example, offers clean rooms, low prices and good service but does not promise expensive furniture or large bathrooms. In contrast, The Ritz-Carlton offers luxurious rooms and a truly memorable experience, but does not promise low prices.

2. See Scott Davis. (2002). *Brand asset management* (2nd ed.). San Francisco, CA: Jossey-Bass. For more on brand positioning, see Philip Kotler & Kevin Lane Keller. (2009). *Marketing management* (13th ed., Chapter 10). Upper Saddle River, NJ: Prentice Hall.
3. Adapted from information found in Geoff Colvin, Selling P&G, *Fortune*, September 17, 2007, pp. 163–169; For P&G, success lies in more than merely a dryer diaper, *Advertising Age*, October 15, 2007, p. 20; Jack Neff, Stengel discusses transition at P&G, *Advertising Age*, July 21, 2008, p. 17; and Elaine Wong, Stengel: Private label, digital change game, *Brandweek*, March 13, 2009, p. 7.

Armstrong, G., Kotler, P., Trifts, V., Buchwitz, L., & Finlayson, P. (2012). Brand strategy and management. In *Marketing: An introduction* (4th Canadian ed., pp. 338–342). Toronto, ON: Pearson Canada.

Use your margin notes to find the answers to the following questions. Compare your answers with those of a classmate. Fill in any gaps you might have.

1 What are some of the characteristics of the best brand names? Give some examples.

_____

_____

_____

_____

2 What are the three levels at which marketers can position their brands? Give an example of a product that is positioned based on values.

_____

_____

_____

_____

3 Choose one of the following brand names to illustrate how the brand is positioned on each of the three levels. For example:

Smart car is a brand that tells the customer the benefits of the product (it communicates its point of difference). It is easy to identify and distinctive. It is memorable. It can be positioned on the level of attributes (consumes less gas), benefits (is more affordable) and values (reduces pollution).

| • BlackBerry | • IKEA | • Swiss National Bank | • Wal-Mart |
| • Hollister clothing | • Pixar | • Walt Disney | |

_____

_____

_____

_____

_____

_____

4 Use the line numbers in this question to identify the missing words in these collocations from the reading.

LINE 4: _brand name_ _____   LINE 8: marketing _____

LINE 4: _____ positioning   LINE 64: _____ attributes

LINE 8: _____ market   LINE 74: _____ benefit

WARM-UP ASSIGNMENT
Write a Short Persuasive Essay

When you receive feedback from your teacher or your class-mates on this Warm-Up Assignment, you will have some information that you can use to improve your writing on the Final Assignment.

For this assignment, you or your teacher will select a brand name to fill in the blank of the essay prompt.

_____ is an example of a well-positioned brand.

Write a short persuasive essay to agree or disagree with the prompt you developed.

A persuasive essay should try to convince others to accept your viewpoint. Refer to the Models Chapter (page 185) to see an example of a persuasive essay and to learn more about how to write one. Use some of the collocations from the early readings in this chapter. Underline the collocations to identify them for your teacher. Try to use parallel structure in your thesis and concluding statements and in any other sentences that list items. Support your statements about brands with examples.

Academic
Survival Skill

Learning Independently

It is difficult to study at an academic level in a second language. You must constantly struggle with course content, which is always complex, as well as language uncertainty. Furthermore, you may have little time to improve your English and successfully complete your degree or diploma. Not only do you need to learn English to accomplish your goals, you also need to learn English fast.

In the same way that a coach helps an elite athlete, your instructors and professors will help you. However, you must complete some of your training on your own. Consider yourself an elite academic athlete struggling to achieve a difficult goal.

Think about the number of hours that you dedicate to studying English in one week. If you are limited to class time and homework periods, you may not be progressing as quickly as you would like. If you believe that your English skills should be progressing faster, think about how you can learn independently.

Successful language learners understand the following key points that allow them to learn quickly. They

- practise, assessing their own strengths and weaknesses;
- make plans to help develop their weakest language skills;
- remain positive—even when faced with frustration;
- know that what they do outside the classroom is as important to their language learning as what they do inside the classroom;
- know that they don't need to be sitting in the library or the classroom to learn a language.

A. In a group of four or five students, discuss ways that you can practise and improve language skills on your own. Write the ideas in your notebook.

B. When you have finished, combine your best ideas with those from other student groups, and discuss them with your teacher. Some ideas are included here to help you.

What you can do to improve your vocabulary skills

- Make a list of words and store them in a mobile electronic device. Colour-code different parts of speech. As you wait for class to begin or the bus to come, review the words on the list—frequently at first, then less frequently as you learn them.
- Subscribe to a free online "word a day" service.

What you can do to improve your reading skills

- Read in English whatever you like to read in your own language. Read mystery novels or sports magazines, or the entertainment, business, technology or travel section of a newspaper.
- Scan the Internet and newspapers for information that interests you.

What you can do to improve your writing skills

- Use the writing tutorial services available to all students on campus.
- Read a short newspaper article several times; then hide it and rewrite the article. When you have finished, compare your version with the original.

C. Think about your language strengths and weaknesses. Decide which areas of skill development you want to improve, and then make a plan. If you learn independently, you will soon notice an improvement.

| VOCABULARY BUILD | In the following table, vocabulary from Reading 3 is listed in the first column, with a definition in the second column. In the third column, write a sentence that demonstrates an understanding of the definition by connecting the word to your own experience. The first one has been done for you as an example. |  |

VOCABULARY	DEFINITION	CONNECT TO YOUR OWN EXPERIENCE
justified* (adj.) in	having an acceptable explanation or reason	Give an example of an action that is justified. *As it was my birthday, I felt justified in not completing my homework.*

VOCABULARY	DEFINITION	CONNECT TO YOUR OWN EXPERIENCE
claim (v.) that	state that something is true even though it is not yet proven	State a claim that your parent might make about you. _____ _____
advocate* (n.) for	someone who publicly supports something	Name a teacher (or other person) who was an advocate for you. _____
government agency (n.)	organization that provides a specific service (For example, the Better Business Bureau is a government agency that protects consumers.)	Give an example of a government agency in your country or in a country you know about. _____ _____
accuse (v.) of	say that you believe someone did something bad (for example, a crime)	What negative impact can you accuse branding of? _____ _____ _____
deceptive (adj.)	intended to make someone believe something that is not true	Give an example of something that is deceptive in its simplicity. _____ _____
obsolescence (n.)/ obsolete (adj.)	state of no longer being useful because something new has been invented	Name a product that is obsolete today. _____ _____
sustainable* (adj.)	able to continue or be maintained for a long time	Many actions designed to protect the environment are referred to as sustainable. Name two environmentally sustainable activities that people practise today. _____ _____
charge (v.)/ charge (n.)	blame someone for an offence	What might roommates charge each other with? _____ _____ _____

VOCABULARY	DEFINITION	CONNECT TO YOUR OWN EXPERIENCE
mark up (v.)	increase the price of something so as to sell it for more than it cost to make (The opposite of *mark up* is *mark down*.)	Name two products that you know retailers mark up.
unintentional (adj.)	not done deliberately or on purpose (The root word of unintentional is *intent*, which means "goal" or "purpose.")	Describe something you might have done unintentionally.
lure (v.)	persuade someone to do something by making it sound exciting or attractive	How could a marketer lure you into a store?
out of stock (adj.)	not available (The opposite of *out of stock* is *in stock*.)	Name something you had wanted to buy but could not because the product was out of stock.
exaggerating (v.)	making something seem better than it is	Make a statement exaggerating the benefits of using this book to learn English.
subtle (adj.)	not easy to notice unless you are paying very close attention	Name a subtle change that occurs when the seasons change.
watchdog (n.)	person or group who works to protect consumers and make sure companies don't do anything illegal	Give an example of a watchdog organization that you know about.
subsequently* (adv.)	occurring after an event in the past, and often as a consequence (The opposite of *subsequently* is *previously*.)	Describe an event in your past and explain what happened subsequently.

* Appears on the Academic Word List

Relating Text Organization to Content

Reading 3 is an excerpt from a chapter in a marketing textbook, and it is carefully organized. Answer the following questions to learn how the reading is organized. An understanding of text organization will allow you to read faster.

1 Read the first paragraph and predict the section headings.

_____

_____

_____

2 Read the second paragraph. Which of the points are used as headings in this reading? Which are not?

_____

_____

_____

_____

3 Predict the authors' opinions about the negative impact of marketing on individual consumers.

_____

_____

_____

4 Read the third paragraph and explain how the listed points are used to organize the next seven paragraphs.

_____

_____

_____

5 How do these first three paragraphs act like a thesis statement for the chapter?

_____

_____

_____

6 The text in each subheading is divided into two parts. Read the first sentence of each paragraph (starting with the section *High costs of distribution*) and state the pattern that the text follows.

_____

_____

_____

7 Which other kind of text might use this pattern of information presentation? Why?

_____

_____

The Negative Consequences of Branding

So far, in this chapter, you have read and written about brand loyalty and brand positioning. However, many people believe there are negative consequences to branding.

In his 2008 book, *Obsessive Branding Disorder: The Business of Illusion and the Illusion of Business*, Lucas Conley presents the astonishing statistic that 94 percent of twenty- and thirty-year-old women in Japan own Louis Vuitton brand products. He states that Louis Vuitton is so popular in that country that the company prices its products (purses, clothing, shoes and luggage) 20 percent higher in Japan than in other countries. He reports that some women in Japan have stated they would give up becoming mothers to better afford Louis Vuitton products.[1]

A. Do you believe that these are negative consequences of branding? Discuss this with your class. List some of the possible negative consequences that might result from branding.

_____

_____

_____

_____

Social Criticisms of Marketing

Marketing receives much criticism. Some of this criticism is justified; much is not. Social critics claim that certain marketing practices hurt individual consumers, society as a whole and other business firms.

5 Marketing's Impact on Individual Consumers

Consumers have many concerns about how well the marketing system serves their interests. Surveys usually show that consumers hold mixed or even slightly unfavourable attitudes towards marketing practices. Consumer advocates, government agencies and other critics have accused marketing of harming consumers through high prices, 10 deceptive practices, high-pressure selling, … unsafe products, planned obsolescence and poor service to disadvantaged consumers. Such questionable marketing practices are not sustainable in terms of long-term consumer or business welfare.

High Prices

Many critics charge that the marketing system causes prices to be higher than they 15 would be under more "sensible" systems. Such high prices are hard to swallow, especially when the economy takes a downturn. Critics point to three factors—high costs of distribution, high advertising and promotion costs and excessive markups.

---

1. Conley, L. (2008). Loyalty beyond reason. In *Obsessive branding disorder: The business of illusion and the Illusion of business* (p. 1). New York, NY: Public Affairs.

High costs of distribution

A long-standing charge is that ... [resellers] mark up prices beyond the value of their
20 services. Critics charge that there are too many intermediaries, that intermediaries are
inefficient or that they provide unnecessary or duplicate services. As a result, distribution
costs too much, and consumers pay for these excessive costs in the form of higher prices.

How do resellers answer these charges? They argue that intermediaries do work that
would otherwise have to be done by manufacturers or consumers. Markups reflect
25 services that consumers themselves want—more convenience, larger stores [greater
variety], more service, longer store hours, return privileges and others. In fact, they
argue, retail competition is so intense that [profit] margins are actually quite low. For
example, after taxes, supermarket chains are typically left with barely 1 percent profit
on their sales. If some resellers try to charge too much relative to the value they add,
30 other resellers will step in with lower prices. Low-price stores such as Walmart, Costco
and other discounters pressure their competitors to operate efficiently and keep their
prices down. In fact, in the wake of the recent recession, only the most efficient retailers
have survived profitably.

High advertising and promotion costs

35 Modern marketing is also accused of pushing up prices to finance heavy advertising
and sales promotion. For example, a few dozen pills of a heavily-promoted brand of
pain reliever sell for the same price as 100 pills of less-promoted brands ... Cosmetics,
detergents, [personal care products] include promotion and packaging costs that can
amount to 40 percent or more of the manufacturer's price to the retailer. Critics charge
40 that much of the packaging and promotion adds only psychological value to the
product rather than functional value.

Marketers respond that advertising does add to product costs, but that it also adds
value by informing potential buyers of the availability and merits of a brand. Brand
name products may cost more, but branding [promises] buyers ... consistent quality.
45 Moreover, consumers can usually buy functional versions of products at lower prices.
However, they want and are willing to pay more for products that also provide psychological benefits—that make them feel wealthy, attractive or special. Also, heavy
advertising and promotion may be necessary for a firm to match competitors' efforts—
the business would lose "share of mind" if it did not match competitive spending.

50 At the same time, companies are cost-conscious about promotion and try to spend
their money wisely. Today's increasingly more [money-wise] consumers are demanding
[real] value for the prices they pay. The continuing shift toward buying store brands
and generics suggest that when it comes to value, consumers want action, not just talk.

Excessive markups

55 Critics also charge that some companies mark up goods excessively. They point to the
drug industry, where a pill [that costs] five cents to make may cost the consumer
two dollars to buy. They point to ... high [prices] for auto
repairs and other services.

Marketers respond that most businesses try to deal fairly
60 with consumers because they want to build customer relationships and repeat business and that most consumer
abuses are unintentional. When shady marketers do take
advantage of consumers, they should be reported to Better
Business Bureaus or to the provincial Consumer Affairs

65 office. Marketers sometimes respond that consumers often don't understand the reasons for high markups. For example, pharmaceutical markups must cover the costs of purchasing, promoting and distributing existing medicines plus the high research and development costs of formulating and testing new medicines. As pharmaceuticals company GlaxoSmithKline states in its ads, "Today's medicines finance tomorrow's miracles."

70 Deceptive Practices

Marketers are sometimes accused of deceptive practices that lead consumers to believe they will get more value than they actually do. Deceptive practices fall into three groups: pricing, promotion and packaging. *Deceptive pricing* includes practices such as falsely advertising "factory" or "wholesale" prices or a large price reduction from a [false] high
75 retail list price. *Deceptive promotion* includes practices such as misrepresenting the products' features or performance or luring the customers to the store for a bargain that is out of stock. *Deceptive packaging* includes exaggerating package contents through subtle design, using misleading labelling or describing size in misleading terms.

The Competition Bureau acts as a watchdog to prevent such practices. In 2009, for
80 example, it brought criminal charges against individuals and companies who formed [an illegal group to keep gas prices artificially high] in Victoriaville, Quebec. It charged The Brick with misleading advertising related to a mail-in-[discount] promotion. The company subsequently cancelled the [promotion] in response to these concerns. It also took action against Edmonton-based Bioenergy Wellness Inc. and its director after
85 [unproven] claims were made online regarding products used to treat or prevent cancer.[1]

… Marketers argue that most companies avoid deceptive practices. Because such practices harm a company's business in the long run, they simply aren't sustainable. Profitable customer relationships are built upon a foundation of value and trust. If consumers do not get what they expect, they will switch to more reliable products. In addition,
90 consumers usually protect themselves from deception. Most consumers recognize a marketer's selling intent and are careful when they buy, sometimes even to the point of not believing completely true product claims.

High Pressure Selling

Salespeople are sometimes accused of high-pressure selling that persuades people to buy
95 goods they had not thought of buying. It is often said that insurance, real estate and used cars are sold, not bought. Salespeople are trained to deliver smooth, [motivating] talks to [encourage] purchase. They sell hard because sales contests promise big prizes to those who sell the most. Similarly, TV infomercial[s] … use "yell and sell" presentations that create a sense of consumer urgency that only those [who are strongest] can resist.

100 But in most cases, marketers have little to gain from high-pressure selling. Such tactics may work in one-time selling situations for short-term gain. However, most selling involves building long-term relationships with valued customers. High-pressure or deceptive selling can do serious damage to such relationships.

---

1. The actions described in this section and others undertaken each year by the Competition Bureau are outlined on its Announcements webpage at http://www.cb-bc.gc.ca/eic/site/cb-bc.nsf/eng/h_02705.html, accessed June 2009.

Adapted from Armstrong, G., Kotler, P., Trifts, V., Buchwitz, L. & Finlayson, P. (2012). Sustainable marketing, social responsibility and ethics. In *Marketing: An introduction* (4th Canadian ed., pp. 80–83). Toronto, ON: Pearson Education Canada.

B. In the following table, write the key phrases the authors use to present the negative impact of marketing and branding, and how marketers answer the charge in the next paragraph(s). Key phrases for the first two sections have been given.

NEGATIVE IMPACT	RESPONSE TO THE NEGATIVE IMPACT
A long-standing charge is that ...	
Modern marketing is also accused of ...	

C. In the second column of the table, note the words that indicate contrast as the authors move from negative to positive points. What other words can be used to present contrasting information?

_____

_____

FINAL ASSIGNMENT
Write a Persuasive Essay

Write a persuasive essay to respond to this statement.

> Intelligent brand positioning can reduce the negative impacts of branding on consumers.

Start with an introduction and a thesis statement presenting your view. Develop your argument with evidence from the readings in this chapter. Try to end with a conclusion that states a solution or a call for action.

In your writing, use some of the collocations that you have learned in this chapter. Use parallel structure where needed, provide examples to support your points and choose accurate vocabulary to express your ideas.

Refer to the Models Chapter (page 185) to see an example of a persuasive essay and to learn more about how to write one.

CHAPTER 5

Philosophies of Medicine

When Steve Jobs was diagnosed with pancreatic cancer in 2003, he spent nine months trying to cure his cancer with alternative medical treatments: he drank juices, modified his diet, used acupuncture, consulted spiritualists and tried treatments he read about on the Internet. Later, he turned to conventional medicine: he had his DNA sequenced, had a liver transplant in 2009 and took typical cancer drugs.

Steve Jobs died in October 2011, leaving the world to question the value and limits of both alternative and conventional systems of medicine.

you will

- learn vocabulary related to various systems of medicine;

- compare systems of medicine to discover their similarities and differences;

- read excerpts to learn about the philosophies behind these medical systems;

- use the academic perspective to demonstrate an objective viewpoint;

- learn about plagiarism and how to avoid it by referencing;

- learn how to organize in-text citations and references;

- write compare and contrast essays.

GEARING UP

A. Working in a small group, rank people you would seek assistance from (1 = most likely; 7 = least likely) under these conditions.

	AN ALLERGIC REACTION	A PERSISTENT FLU	A BROKEN LEG
The family doctor (sometimes called *General Practitioner* or *GP*)			
The salesperson at the health food store			
A family member			
The pharmacist at the drugstore			
The healer you found online			
A naturopathic doctor (who may use herbal medicine or acupuncture)			
A doctor at a hospital			

B. Discuss your top- and bottom-ranked people for each condition with group members. Can you explain any difference in rankings among the members of your group? What medical training do you hope people have before they give you advice about these (relatively) minor health issues?

Conventional and Complementary and Alternative Medicine

The definitions in this reading have been taken from the National Center for Complementary and Alternative Medicine (NCCAM) website. NCCAM is the U.S. government's lead agency for scientific research on health care systems that are not generally included in conventional medicine.

Read the definitions. When you have finished, demonstrate your understanding by writing the words that follow under the correct heading in the table: either conventional medicine or complementary and alternative medicine.

Conventional medicine (also known as Western, mainstream or biomedicine) is practised by holders of MD (medical doctor) or DO (Doctor of Osteopathic Medicine) degrees and by allied health professionals such as physical therapists, psychologists and registered nurses.

Complementary and alternative medicine (CAM) is a group of diverse medical and health care systems, practices and products that are not presently considered part of conventional medicine. Complementary medicine is used together with conventional medicine, and alternative medicine is used in the place of conventional medicine. The boundaries between CAM and conventional medicine are not absolute, and specific CAM practices may, over time, become widely accepted.

National Center for Complementary and Alternative Medicine. (2011, July). What Is complementary and alternative medicine? Retrieved from: http://nccam.nih.gov/

"Ayurveda" is the traditional Indian medical practice of treating mind, body and spirit as one. "Qigong" is the Chinese medical practice of aligning physical postures, breathing and mental focus.

acupuncture	Eastern	surgery
antibiotics	qigong	traditional Chinese medicine
ayurveda	herbal medicine	vaccination
biomedicine	pharmaceutical drugs	vitamin supplements
blood tests	prayer	Western
chemotherapy	radiation	yoga

CONVENTIONAL MEDICINE	COMPLEMENTARY AND ALTERNATIVE MEDICINE
surgery	yoga

A. Working with another student, match the type of practitioner in the left column to what he or she does in the right column. The first one has been done for you. When you have finished, confirm your answers with the class.

B. Discuss the use of the verbs *treat* and *perform* in relation to doctors. When do you use each verb?

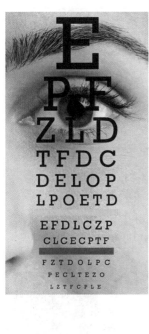

TYPE OF PRACTITIONER	WHAT THE PRACTITIONER DOES
① dentist	__1__ treats a patient's teeth
② optometrist	_____ treats pain by manipulating bones and muscles
③ surgeon	_____ treats pain by manipulating muscles and suggesting specific exercises
④ chiropractor	_____ treats a disease by exposing the patient to small amounts of the substance that causes the disease
⑤ physical therapist	_____ treats pain by massaging muscles
⑥ homeopath	_____ treats a patient's eyes and orders glasses or contact lenses
⑦ herbalist	_____ treats pain by inserting small needles into a patient's body
⑧ acupuncturist	_____ pretends to be a doctor (term showing strong disapproval)
⑨ massage therapist	_____ performs operations in a hospital
⑩ quack	_____ treats diseases with medicine made from plants

C. As you might recall, collocations are words that often appear together in recognized mini-expressions (see page 74). The following chart displays collocations with the words *doctor* and *practitioner*.

VERB	NOUN
see	a/the doctor
go to	
visit	a practitioner
consult	a medical practitioner

Identify the different kind of doctor or type of practitioner you would need in each of the following situations. Use the correct collocation in your answer.

① You have a pain in your shoulder or knee.

I would visit a physical therapist.

② You have a sore back.

_____

▶

3 You have a cold.

_____

4 You have stomach trouble.

_____

5 You feel tired all the time.

_____

6 You have allergies.

_____

7 You break a bone.

_____

8 You feel anxious or stressed.

_____

D. Discuss what happens when you are treated for these kinds of health problems. Do you think the treatment is effective; does it make you feel better?

E. There are many possible word forms relating to doctors and the medicine they practise. Fill in the chart below to learn some of these word forms. The first one is given as an example.

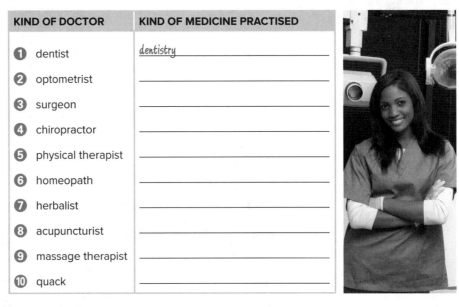

KIND OF DOCTOR	KIND OF MEDICINE PRACTISED
1 dentist	_dentistry_
2 optometrist	_____
3 surgeon	_____
4 chiropractor	_____
5 physical therapist	_____
6 homeopath	_____
7 herbalist	_____
8 acupuncturist	_____
9 massage therapist	_____
10 quack	_____

READING ❷ Complementary and Alternative Medicine

A. Read the descriptions of four systems of complementary and alternative medicine (CAM). After reading about each system of CAM, write short notes in the chart following the description. These notes will help you see the similarities and differences between the different forms of CAM. When you have finished, compare your notes with a classmate's to confirm your comprehension.

Four Systems of CAM

1. Traditional Chinese Medicine

Traditional Chinese medicine (TCM) originated in ancient China and has evolved over thousands of years. TCM practitioners use herbs, acupuncture and other methods to

5 treat a wide range of conditions. In the Western world, TCM is considered part of complementary and alternative medicine (CAM).

10 **Background:** Traditional Chinese medicine, which encompasses many different practices, is rooted in the ancient philosophy 15 of Taoism and dates back more than 5,000 years. Today, TCM is practised side by side with Western medicine in many of China's hospitals and clinics: … TCM is widely used in the Western world.

20 **Underlying Concepts:** Underlying the practice of TCM is a unique view of the world and the human body that is different from Western medicine concepts. This view is based on the ancient Chinese perception of humans as microcosms of the larger, surrounding universe—interconnected with nature and subject to its forces. The human body is regarded as an organic entity in which the various organs, tissues 25 and other parts have distinct functions but are all interdependent. In this view, health and disease relate to balance of the functions.

The theoretical framework of TCM has a number of key components:

- Yin/yang theory—the concept of two opposing, yet complementary, forces that shape the world and all life—is central to TCM.

30 • In the TCM view, a vital energy or life force called *qi* circulates in the body through a system of pathways called *meridians*. Health is an ongoing process of maintaining balance and harmony in the circulation of qi.

- The TCM approach uses eight principles to analyze symptoms and categorize conditions: cold/heat, interior/exterior, excess/deficiency and yin/yang (the chief princi-35 ples). TCM also uses the theory of five elements—fire, earth, metal, water and wood—to explain how the body works; these elements correspond to particular organs and tissues in the body.

…

Treatment: TCM emphasizes individualized treatment. Practitioners traditionally used four methods to evaluate a patient's condition: observing (especially the tongue), 40 hearing/smelling, asking/interviewing and touching/palpating (especially the pulse).

TCM practitioners use a variety of therapies in an effort to promote health and treat disease. The most commonly used are Chinese herbal medicine and acupuncture.

- Chinese herbal medicine: The Chinese *Material Medica* (a pharmacological reference book used by TCM practitioners) contains hundreds of medicinal substances—pri-45 marily plants, but also some minerals and animal products—classified by their perceived action in the body. Different parts of plants such as the leaves, roots, stems, flowers and seeds are used. Usually, herbs are combined in formulas and given as teas, capsules, tinctures or powders.

- Acupuncture: By stimulating specific points on the body, most often by inserting
50 thin metal needles through the skin, practitioners seek to remove blockages in the
flow of qi.

Other TCM therapies include moxibustion (burning moxa—a cone or stick of dried
herb, usually mugwort—on or near the skin, sometimes in conjunction with acupuncture); cupping (applying a heated cup to the skin to create a slight suction); Chinese
55 massage; mind-body therapies such as qigong and tai chi; and dietary therapy.

TRADITIONAL CHINESE MEDICINE	NOTES
PHILOSOPHY: What is the main idea, approach or theory?	
METHOD: What do the practitioners actually do?	
YOUR THOUGHTS: Do you think this system is effective? Explain your answer.	

2. Homeopathy

Homeopathy, also known as homeopathic medicine, is a whole medical system that
was developed in Germany more than 200 years ago and has been practised in the
Western world since the early nineteenth century. Homeopathy is used for wellness
60 and prevention and to treat many diseases and conditions.

Overview: The term homeopathy comes from the Greek words *homeo*, meaning "similar," and *pathos*, meaning "suffering or disease." Homeopathy seeks to stimulate the
body's ability to heal itself by giving very small doses of highly diluted substances. This
therapeutic method was developed by German physician Samuel Christian Hahnemann
65 at the end of the eighteenth century. Hahnemann articulated two main principles.

- The principle of similar (or "like cures like") states that a disease can be cured by a
substance that produces similar symptoms in healthy people. This idea, which can
be traced back to Hippocrates, was further developed by Hahnemann after he
repeatedly ingested cinchona bark, a popular treatment for malaria, and found that
70 he developed the symptoms of the disease. Hahnemann theorized that if a substance
could cause disease symptoms in a healthy person, small amounts could cure a sick
person who had similar symptoms.

- The principle of dilutions (or "law of minimum dose") states that the lower the dose
of the medication, the greater its effectiveness. In homeopathy, substances are
75 diluted in a stepwise fashion and shaken vigorously between each dilution. This
process, referred to as "potentization," is believed to transmit some form of information or energy from the original substance to the final diluted remedy. Most
homeopathic remedies are so dilute that no molecules of the healing substance
remain; however, in homeopathy, it is believed that the substance has left its imprint
80 or "essence," which stimulates the body to heal itself (this theory is called the
"memory of water").

Homeopaths treat people based on genetic and personal health history, body type
and current physical, emotional and mental symptoms. Patient visits tend to be
lengthy. Treatments are "individualized" or tailored to each person—it is not uncommon
85 for different people with the same condition to receive different treatments.

Homeopathic remedies are derived from natural substances that come from plants, minerals or animals. Common remedies include red onion, arnica (mountain herb) and stinging nettle plant.

HOMEOPATHY	NOTES
PHILOSOPHY: What is the main idea, approach or theory?	
METHOD: What do the practitioners actually do?	
YOUR THOUGHTS: Do you think this system is effective? Explain your answer.	

3. Naturopathy

90 Naturopathy, also called naturopathic medicine, is a whole medical system—one of the systems of healing and beliefs that have evolved over time in different cultures and parts of the world. Naturopathy is rooted in health care approaches that were popular in Europe, and includes therapies (both ancient and modern) from many traditions. In naturopathy, the emphasis is on supporting health rather than combatting disease.

95 **A Brief Description of Naturopathy:** Naturopathy is a whole medical system that has its roots in Germany. It was developed further in the late nineteenth and early twentieth centuries in the Western world, where today it is part of complementary and alternative medicine (CAM). The word naturopathy comes from Greek and Latin and literally translates as "nature disease."

100 A central belief in naturopathy is that nature has a healing power (a principle called *vis medicatrix naturae*). Another belief is that living organisms (including the human body) have the power to maintain (or return to) a state of balance and health and to heal themselves. Practitioners of naturopathy prefer to use treatment approaches that they consider to be the most natural and least invasive, instead of using drugs and more 105 invasive procedures.

Key Principles: The practice of naturopathy is based on six key principles:

1. Promote the healing power of nature.

2. First, do no harm. Naturopathic practitioners choose therapies with the intent to keep harmful side effects to a minimum and not
110 suppress symptoms.

3. Treat the whole person. Practitioners believe a person's health is affected by many factors, such as physical, mental, emotional, genetic, environmental and social ones. Practitioners consider all these factors when choosing therapies and tailor treatment
115 to each patient.

4. Treat the cause. Practitioners seek to identify and treat the causes of a disease or condition, rather than its symptoms. They believe that symptoms are signs
120 that the body is trying to fight disease, adapt to it or recover from it.

5. Prevention is the best cure. Practitioners teach ways of living that they consider most healthy and most likely to prevent illness.

125 6. The physician is a teacher. Practitioners consider it important to educate their patients in taking responsibility for their own health.

NATUROPATHY	NOTES
PHILOSOPHY: What is the main idea, approach or theory?	
METHOD: What do the practitioners actually do?	
YOUR THOUGHTS: Do you think this system is effective? Explain your answer.	

4. Chiropractic

Chiropractic is a health care approach that focuses on the relationship between the body's structure—mainly the spine—and its functioning. Although practitioners may
130 use a variety of treatment approaches, they primarily perform adjustments to the spine or other parts of the body with the goal of correcting alignment problems and supporting the body's natural ability to heal itself.

Overview and History: The term chiropractic combines the Greek words *cheir* (hand) and *praxis* (action) to describe a treatment done by hand. Hands-on therapy—espe-
135 cially adjustment of the spine—is central to chiropractic care. Chiropractic, which in the Western world is considered part of complementary and alternative medicine (CAM), is based on these key concepts:

• The body has a powerful self-healing ability.

• The body's structure (primarily that of the spine) and its function are closely related,
140 and this relationship affects health.

• Therapy aims to normalize this relationship between structure and function and assist the body as it heals.

What to Expect from Chiropractic Visits: During the initial visit, chiropractors typically take a health history and perform a physical examination, with a special
145 emphasis on the spine. Other examinations or tests such as x-rays may also be performed. If chiropractic treatment is considered appropriate, a treatment plan will be developed.

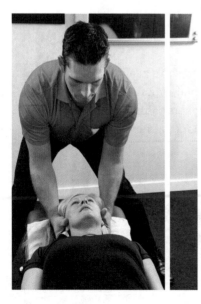

During follow-up visits, practitioners may perform one or more of the many different types of adjustments used in chiropractic care. Given mainly to
150 the spine, a chiropractic adjustment (sometimes referred to as a manipulation) involves using the hands or a device to apply a controlled, sudden force to a joint, moving it beyond its passive range of motion. The goal is to increase the range and quality of motion in the area being treated and to aid in restoring health. Other hands-on therapies such as mobilization
155 (movement of a joint within its usual range of motion) may also be used.

Chiropractors may combine the use of spinal adjustments with several other treatments and approaches, such as heat and ice; electrical stimulation; rest; rehabilitative exercise; counselling about diet, weight loss and other lifestyle factors; and dietary supplements.

CHIROPRACTIC	NOTES
PHILOSOPHY: What is the main idea, approach or theory?	
METHOD: What do the practitioners actually do?	
YOUR THOUGHTS: Do you think this system is effective? Explain your answer.	

Sutton, A. L. (Ed.). (2010). *Complementary and alternative medicine sourcebook* (4th ed., pp. 74-76; pp. 85-86; pp. 91-93; pp. 399-401). Detroit, MI: Omnigraphics Inc.

B. With a partner or in a small group, discuss the similarities and differences between the four forms of CAM. In order to express your ideas clearly, use your knowledge of conjunctions and sentence structure (from the Focus on Writing, pages 36–39). Refer to the chart below for help.

TYPE OF CONJUNCTION	TO EXPRESS SIMILARITY	TO EXPRESS CONTRAST
subordinate	as/just as	although/even if/even though/though/whereas/while
coordinate	and	but yet
adverbial	likewise similarly	however nevertheless

In addition to conjunctions

	compared to/with in comparison parallel to	in contrast to as opposed to unlike

C. Write four sentences to demonstrate the similarities and differences between various forms of CAM. Show your sentences to either a classmate or your teacher. Check to make sure that your sentence structure is correct.

> Example: While traditional Chinese medicine has been tested over thousands of years, homeopathy was developed in Germany over the last 200 years. (DC, IC).

❶ _____

_____

❷ _____

_____

❸ _____

_____

❹ _____

_____

Considering the Academic Perspective

When you use the academic perspective you should always be *objective*. This means that when you want to speak or write in a formal academic manner, you must present the facts. Your experiences and opinions are less useful because they are *subjective*: that is, based on your feelings and emotions—not the facts.

Sometimes, your instructors may ask you to speak or write about a personal experience or to express a view based on your opinions; in these cases, it is acceptable to write about yourself and what you think. However, as you progress in your post-secondary education, your instructors will ask you to read and summarize other sources of information. You will need to base these assignments on information that is objective. You will no longer be able to use your experiences or opinions to support the statements in these assignments.

Avoiding the personal perspective in academic writing isn't hard if you know how to revise sentences that are subjective. Look at the following examples.

PERSONAL PERSPECTIVE/ FIRST PERSON/SUBJECTIVE	ACADEMIC PERSPECTIVE/ THIRD PERSON/OBJECTIVE
I think that acupuncture is a good technique to relieve pain.	Acupuncture is a technique used to relieve pain.
In my opinion, alternative and complementary medicines are different approaches to health care.	Alternative and complementary medicines are different approaches to health care.
Once I went to see a chiropractor, and he really helped me understand that my poor posture was causing problems for my digestive system.	Chiropractors can help people understand how a poorly aligned spine influences other systems in the body. For example, poor posture may cause problems for the digestive system.
My father always took me to see a homeopathic doctor for my allergies because he believed children shouldn't be given needles or drugs for allergy problems.	Many people visit homeopathic doctors in order to avoid injections or drugs as treatment.
I know many more people are visiting alternative doctors than ever before.	Seventy-four percent of all Canadians report they have used an alternative therapy at some point in their lives.[1]

Convert these sentences from a subjective perspective to an objective perspective. Use information from the articles in Reading 2.

1. I never believed a chiropractic doctor could help reduce my back pain—until I went to see one.

   _____

   _____

2. In my opinion, acupuncture can help many people.

   _____

   _____

---

1. Esmail, N. (2007). Complementary and alternative medicine in Canada: Trends in use and public attitudes, 1997–2006. *Public Policy Sources, No. 87,* p. 4. Vancouver, BC: The Fraser Institute.

3 I was hoping ginseng would make me smarter for my exams, but it didn't help me at all.

_____

_____

4 Like more and more people these days, I suffer from allergies.

_____

_____

5 My homeopath says that the body has an innate ability to heal itself.

_____

_____

WARM-UP ASSIGNMENT
Write a Short Compare and Contrast Essay

Write a short compare and contrast essay. In order to keep the essay relatively short, review the four systems of CAM in Reading 2, and select two of them. Decide whether you will write about their similarities or their differences.

In a compare and contrast essay, you must organize and explain the similarities or differences that you identify. Refer to the Models Chapter (page 187) to see an example of a compare and contrast essay and learn more about how to write one. Be sure to write from an academic perspective. Use parallel structure when necessary.

> *When you receive feedback from your teacher or your class-mates on this Warm-Up Assignment, you will have some information that you can use to improve your writing on the Final Assignment.*

VOCABULARY BUILD

A. Read the following sentences from Reading 3 and write a definition for the words in bold. Use clues in the sentence to help you, or use your dictionary. When you have finished, confirm your definitions with the class.

WORDS IN CONTEXT	DEFINITION
1 The best treatment, selected by the physician, is based on statistical **analysis*** of data **obtained*** from randomized clinical trials.	analysis: *detailed examination*
	obtained:
2 The physician is the **authority*** figure with the knowledge and power to save the patient.	authority:

WORDS IN CONTEXT	DEFINITION
3 There is often little, if any, room in the biomedical model for the intuitive or emotional **dimensions*** of either the physician or patient, and medical knowledge is therefore generally impersonal.	dimensions:
4 Some practitioners of modern medicine have proposed over the past several decades humanistic **modifications*** of the biomedical model, in order to emphasize the humanity of both patient and physician in medical knowledge and practice.	modifications:
5 The biomedical world view is modified in humanistic or humane models, which suggest the person is composed of two non-reducible **entities***—the body and the mind.	entities:
6 Although the humanistic or humane models share many **features*** with the biomedical model, they also rely on a practitioner's emotions and intuitions.	features:
7 Once **identified*** by objective diagnostic procedures, treatment is generally based on some type of drug or surgical procedure.	identified:
8 According to the biomedical model, the patient is a machine composed of **individual*** body parts that, when broken or lost, can be fixed or replaced by new parts.	individual:
9 Moreover, the patient is not simply a **passive*** agent during diagnosis or treatment but can also be an active participant.	passive:
10 Instead of the physician being **rationally*** concerned in an emotionally detached manner for the patient's diseased body part, the humanistic or humane **practitioner*** cares both rationally and emotionally for the health of the patient ... as a ... person. The underlying value of this type of medical practice is **empathy**.	rationally:
	practitioner:
	empathy:

WORDS IN CONTEXT	DEFINITION
⑪ The acquisition and **implementation*** of medical knowledge reflects the techniques and **procedures*** of these sciences.	implementation:
	procedures:
⑫ The patient as an informed agent is part of the **process*** of humanistic medicine.	process:
⑬ Medical practice within the biomedical model is based on objective or scientific knowledge and **relies*** on the technological developments in the natural sciences, especially the biomedical sciences.	relies:
⑭ Although the biomedical model has provided major advances, one of its chief **underlying*** problems is the **alienation** of the patient from the physician.	underlying:
	alienation:

* Appears on the Academic Word List

B. These sentences contain some of the main points from Reading 3. Once you have confirmed the definitions with the class, use this vocabulary to predict the content of the reading.

READING ③ More Medical Models

While there have been many advances in health care that are attributable to Western medicine, this does not mean that the Western model of medicine is not without problems. In Reading 3, the author contrasts Western and humanistic models of medicine to argue for a more humane model of health care in which the doctor considers the emotional, social and spiritual lives of patients as well as their physical bodies.

A. Read the text and divide it into four main sections by listing the line number at the end of each section. When you have finished, confirm your section divisions with the class. The four section headings are:

❶ Definitions of Western and humanistic models   ENDS LINE: _____

❷ Patient as physical entity OR physical and emotional entity   ENDS LINE: _____

❸ Medicine based on science OR on science and intuition ENDS LINE: _____

❹ Doctor as authority figure OR empathetic figure   ENDS LINE: _____

Western and Humanistic Models of Medicine

Today, the biomedical model is the prevailing model of medical knowledge and practice within ... Western and other developed countries, and it is also becoming the dominant model in Eastern and underdeveloped countries. In this model, the patient
5 is reduced to a physical body composed of separate body parts that occupy a machine-world. The physician's emotionally detached concern is to identify the patient's diseased body part and to treat or replace it, using the latest scientific and technological advances in medical knowledge ... approved ... by the medical community. The outcome of this intervention is to cure the patient, thereby saving the patient from
10 permanent injury or possibly death.

Although the biomedical model has provided major advances ..., one of its chief underlying problems is the alienation of the patient from the physician. "The public perceives medicine," claims Miles Little, "to be too impersonal" (1995, p. 2). Moreover, by reducing the patient to a collection of body parts, the patient as a person disap-
15 pears before the physician's clinical gaze (MacIntyre, 1979). The loss of the patient as a person from the physician's clinical gaze has led to a quality-of-care crisis, which afflicts ... Western ... medicine today, and has eroded the intimacy of today's patient-physician relationship from a perceived intimacy of an earlier age ...[1] For example, much of the infrastructure supporting current ... Western ... medical practice favours
20 the physician's schedule at the expense of the patient's lifestyle and at times the patient's health and well-being. Importantly, Engel identified the origins of this crisis in the "adherence to a [biomedical] model of disease no longer adequate for the scientific tasks and social responsibilities of either medicine or psychiatry" (1977, p. 129). In other words, the crisis arose over ... ignoring ... the psychological and
25 social dimensions associated with the patient's experience of illness and the physician's inability to understand the patient as an ill *person*.

In response to the quality-of-care crisis, some practitioners of modern medicine have proposed over the past several decades humanistic modifications of the biomedical model, in order to ... emphasize the humanity of both patient and physician in medical
30 knowledge and practice. Michael Schwartz and Osborne Wiggins broadly define humanistic or humane medicine accordingly: "medical practice that focuses on the whole person and not solely on the patient's disease" (1988, p. 159).They do not reject scientific medicine but enlarge its scope to include the patient's psychological and social dimensions. Davis-Floyd and St. John concur with this assessment of the
35 humanistic models: "Humanists wish simply to humanize ... biomedicine—that is, to make it relational, partnership-oriented, individually responsive and compassionate" (1998, p. 82) ...

In humanistic models, the patient is recognized as a person ... or at least an organism composed of body and mind occupying a lived context or a socio-economic environ-
40 ment. Under the practitioner's empathic gaze and care, the informed and autonomous patient is cured and at times even healed using generally scientific evidence-based or traditional medical therapies but possibly—and then only as a last resort—non-traditional therapies.

---

1. Of course, humanistic or humane practitioners do not reject the advances of the biomedical model for a myth that medicine prior to it was somehow better because of the intimacy between the patient and physician (Engel, 1977, p. 135).

According to the biomed
45 ical model, the patient is a
machine composed of
individual body parts that,
when broken or lost, can
be fixed or replaced by
50 new parts. Moreover, disease, whose cause can be
identified by scientific
analysis, is an objective
entity. It is often organic
55 and seldom, if ever, psychological or mental. The
notion of health involves
the absence of disease or
the normal functioning of
60 body parts. Physicians are
interested in identifying
only the physical causes or

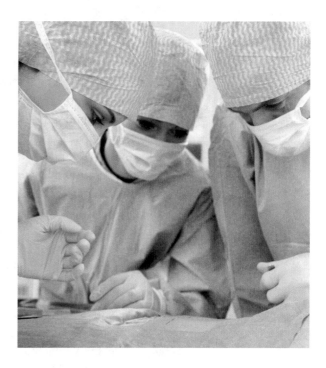

entities that are responsible for a patient's disease. Once identified by objective
diagnostic procedures, treatment is generally based on some type of drug or surgical
65 procedure. … The best treatment …, selected by the physician, is based on statistical
analysis of data obtained from randomized clinical trials. Thus, the physician is a
mechanic or technician, whose task is to determine which part of a patient's body
is broken or diseased and to mend or replace it.

The biomedical world view is modified in humanistic or humane models, which
70 suggest the person is … composed of two non-reducible entities—the body and the
mind. Other humanistic models operate from a holistic position, in which the person
(or self) represents an integrated whole not only in terms of the individual but with
the person's environmental … and social contexts. Although practitioners of humanistic models of medical knowledge and practice appreciate the biomedical model's
75 … position of reductionism and the gains it provides for the technical side of Western
medicine, they often reject it as an insufficient presupposition for medical knowledge
and practice. They generally … believe that people are not defined by their … individual parts but transcend them. Practitioners of humanistic models … include …
the patient's psychological or mental state—and for some, the spiritual state.

80 Instead of reducing the patient to the physical body alone, the humanistic or humane
practitioner, who is not just a mechanic, encounters the patient as a person composed of both mind and body. Importantly, the mind and body often influence the
behaviour and state of each other in a reciprocal manner. Thus, the mind and body
are complementary aspects of the patient, and both must be considered when
85 making a diagnosis or choosing a therapy. For the patient's illness may be more
than simply organic (a disease) but may also include the psychological and social
(an illness or a sickness, respectively). Causation then is more than physical …
Moreover, rather than being considered just a machine composed of individual parts
separate from any background or framework, the patient is viewed as an organism
90 or a person within a socioeconomic environment or cultural background. And as
an organism or a person the patient is more than simply the sum of separate body
parts but also exhibits properties that surpass the aggregation of those parts …

Medical practice within the biomedical model is based on objective or scientific knowledge and relies on the technological developments in the natural sciences,
95 especially the biomedical sciences. The acquisition and implementation of medical knowledge reflects the techniques and procedures of these sciences. For example, the randomized, double-blind, concurrently controlled trial is considered the primary or "gold" standard for determining the efficacy of a new drug or surgical procedure. Such scientific practice defines acceptable knowledge and practice of medicine within
100 the biomedical model. Medical knowledge in this model is generally based on mechanistic causation. Finally, … medical … claims in the biomedical model depend on the logical relationship of … statements obtained from … laboratory experiments and clinical studies. The trajectory of medical knowledge and practice is from the laboratory to the bedside. There is often little, if any, room in this model for the intui-
105 tive or emotional dimensions of either the physician or patient, and medical knowledge is therefore generally impersonal.

Although the humanistic or humane models share many … features with the biomedical model, they also rely on a practitioner's emotions and intuitions. Emotions and intuitions are not necessarily impediments to sound medical judgment and
110 practice; but when judiciously utilized and constrained by … the boundaries of the biomedical model, they enable a physician to access information about a patient's illness that may exceed quantified data, e.g., laboratory test results. This information obtained from a practitioner's use of emotional and intuitional resources is subjective and human. Behind such information is the face of the "Other" (Tauber, 1995). The
115 type of knowledge obtained in this model depends on … a patient's psychosocial dimension and … is an important factor in diagnosing and treating illness. Moreover, the patient is not simply a passive agent during diagnosis or treatment but can also be an active participant. The patient as an informed agent is part of the process of humanistic medicine.

120 The biomedical model stresses the scientific problem-solving aspect of medical practice and is based on a value of objectivity. Diagnosis and treatment of a patient's disease are puzzles that concern the physician-scientist … as a … mechanic or technician. Diagnosis of the disease depends on a technology that reduces the patient to a set of objective data, from which the physician diagnoses the patient's disease. And
125 from that diagnosis, the physician then chooses the appropriate … treatment …, often with little patient consultation. The ethical stance of the physician is a concern to save the patient from the disease and ultimately from death. According to the biomedical model, death is defeat and is generally avoided at all costs. The physician's concern for the patient is detached from the emotions of both the physician and
130 patient. Moreover, the patient's relationship to a physician is passive. The physician is the authority figure with the knowledge and power to save the patient. Thus, the physician's relationship to a patient is one of dominance, as represented by paternalism.

Instead of the physician being rationally concerned in an emotionally detached
135 manner for the patient's diseased body part, the humanistic or humane practitioner cares both rationally and emotionally for the health of the patient … as a … person. The underlying value of this type of medical practice is empathy. … With empathy …, the physician may become aware of … other … features of a patient's illness, including losses of wholeness, certainty, control, freedom to act and the familiar world
140 (Toombs, 1993). The physician is no longer the … supreme authority and power in

curing a patient but a first among equals, a co-participant with a patient and other healthcare providers. In other words, the patient 145 is an autonomous person who deserves respect for helping to make the choice as to how to proceed therapeutically. Moreover, the physician recognizes that a 150 patient's mind/body often cures itself and that often the role of both the physician and patient is to assist in that process and not to hinder it. The patient-physician 155 relationship is one of mutual respect, for the role and contribution of each other in the healing process. Finally, death is not necessarily a defeat according to this 160 model but another or possibly final stage in the patient's life.

References

Davis-Floyd, R., & St. John, G. (1998). *From doctor to healer: The transformative journey.* New Brunswick, NJ: Rutgers University Press.

Engel, G.L. (1977, April 8). The need for a new medical model: A challenge for biomedicine. *Science, 196*, 129–136.

Little, M. (1995). *Human medicine.* Cambridge, UK: Cambridge University Press.

MacIntyre, A. (1979). Medicine aimed at the care of persons rather than what …? In J. Cassell, & Siegler. M. (Eds.), *Changing values in medicine* (pp. 83–96). Frederick, MD: Unlimited Publications of America.

Schwartz, M.A., & Wiggins, O.P. (1988). Scientific and humanistic medicine. In K.L. White (Ed.), *The task of medicine: Dialogue at Wickenburg* (pp. 137–171). Menlo Park, CA: Henry J. Kaiser Family Foundation.

Tauber, A.I. (1995). From the self to the other: Building a philosophy of medicine. In M.A. Grodin (Ed.), *Meta medical ethics: The philosophical foundations of bioethics* (pp. 158–195). Dordrecht, The Netherlands: Kluwer.

Toombs, S.K. (1993). *The meaning of illness: A phenomenological account of the different perspectives of physician and patient.* Dordrecht, The Netherlands: Kluwer.

Marcum, J. (2008). *Humanizing modern medicine: An introductory philosophy of medicine* (pp. 8–13). Dordrecht, The Netherlands: Springer.

B. Answer the questions about each section to demonstrate your comprehension of the text. When you have finished, compare your answers with a classmate's.

Section 1

❶ According to this author, what are the characteristics of the Western or biomedical model of medicine?

_____

_____

_____

_____

_____

▶

2 According to this author, what are the characteristics of the humanistic model of medicine?

_____

_____

_____

_____

_____

Section 2

3 What metaphor is used to describe the patient in the biomedical model of medicine? What is the role of the doctor in this model? How do you feel about this?

_____

_____

_____

_____

4 How does the humanistic model of medicine view the patient, and what is the role of the doctor in this model?

_____

_____

_____

_____

_____

Section 3

5 What must be the origin of all medical knowledge in the biomedical model of medicine?

_____

_____

_____

_____

6 Does the humanistic doctor value scientific knowledge? How are a doctor's emotions and intuitions regarded in the humanistic model of medicine?

_____

_____

_____

7 What is the role of the patient in the humanistic model of medicine?

_____

_____

_____

8 Describe the patient-doctor relationship in the biomedical model of medicine.

_____

_____

_____

_____

9 Describe the patient-doctor relationship in the humanistic model of medicine.

_____

_____

_____

_____

FOCUS ON READING

Recognizing a Compare and Contrast Text

Study the organization of Reading 3 to answer these questions about compare and contrast text structure.

A. Complete the table below to create an outline of the reading.

SECTION	MODEL OF MEDICINE IN ORDER OF APPEARANCE IN THE TEXT
❶ Definitions of Western and humanistic models	**❶** _biomedical model_ **❷** _humanistic model_
❷ Patient as physical entity OR physical and emotional entity	**❶** _____ **❷** _____
❸ Medicine based on science OR on science and intuition	**❶** _____ **❷** _____
❹ Doctor as authority figure OR empathetic figure	**❶** _____ **❷** _____

B. Write the first clause or phrase of the sentence(s) the author uses to switch from writing about one model to writing about the next model within each section. The first one has been done for you.

SECTION 1: _In response to the quality-of-care crisis, ..._____

SECTION 2: _____

SECTION 3: _____

SECTION 4: _____

Notice how the author uses the initial clause or phrase of the topic sentence(s) to signal the switch of content to the reader. When you write a compare and contrast essay, try to do the same.

Avoiding Plagiarism by Referencing

Copying another person's words or ideas is called *plagiarism*, and it is considered an academic "crime." As there are serious academic penalties for students who plagiarize, plagiarism should be of significant concern for students and instructors alike.

Generally, there are two types of plagiarism:

• copying another person's *words*

• copying another person's *ideas*

Providing in-text citations and references for other people's words and ideas is one way to avoid plagiarizing. When you give a reference, you let the reader know who originally wrote or said the referenced words or who developed the referenced ideas.

You have seen in-text citations and references before; in fact, there are a number of them in this book. In-text citations and references are the paper equivalents of embedded electronic links. They allow the reader to find the original source.

• In-text citations (found in the body of a text) briefly identify *the original author* of the words or ideas you are writing about *and the date* on which the work was published without interrupting the flow of the reading. For each in-text citation, you need to have complete information about the publication in a reference section or in a bibliography.

• References (found at the end of a text or in a bibliography) should provide enough detail so that readers can find the source of the words or ideas you are writing about.

Citing and referencing words and ideas is easy; however, citing and referencing them accurately can be challenging. To confuse matters further, there are a number of different citation and referencing styles, such as

• American Psychological Association (APA)

• Modern Languages Association (MLA)

• Institute for Electrical and Electronics Engineers (IEEE)

Each style demands that citation and reference elements be placed in a specific order with unique punctuation.

The in-text citation and reference examples in the following section are formatted according to American Psychological Association (APA) require-ments. As APA format is widely used in the social sciences, this style of citing and referencing will be useful for many students.

In-Text Citations

Examples of in-text citations when a writer uses another writer's words.

	EXAMPLE	CHARACTERISTICS
LINE 12	"The public perceives medicine," claims Miles Little, "to be too impersonal" (1995, p. 2).	• short quotation • use of quotation marks • author name in the text • date and page number at the end in parentheses
LINE 21	Importantly, Engel identified the origins of this crisis in the "adherence to a [biomedical] model of disease no longer adequate for the scientific tasks and social responsibilities of either medicine or psychiatry" (1977, p. 129).	
LINE 30	Michael Schwartz and Osborne Wiggins broadly define humanistic or humane medicine accordingly: "medical practice that focuses on the whole person and not solely on the patient's disease" (1988, p. 159).	

Examples of in-text citations when a writer uses another writer's ideas.

	EXAMPLE	CHARACTERISTICS
LINE 13	Moreover, by reducing the patient to a collection of body parts, the patient as a person disappears before the physician's clinical gaze (MacIntyre, 1979).	• NOT a quotation • ideas are paraphrased • author and date in parentheses at end
LINE 138	... the physician may become aware of ... other ... features of a patient's illness, including losses of wholeness, certainty, control, freedom to act and the familiar world (Toombs, 1993).	• page number NOT included, likely because this idea is a main idea of the original author and repeated in more than one place

A Note on Referencing Another Writer's Ideas

Using another writer's ideas without referencing them is considered plagiarism. Here are some general guidelines to help you avoid using another person's ideas improperly.

Writing about information that is considered general knowledge in your field is *not* considered plagiarism.

> Example: Scientists have made great progress in their understanding of how physical problems are related to depression.

This isn't considered copying another person's ideas because it is a widely known fact in the field of medicine. Many researchers have agreed that this is true, and many people have written about this idea in a variety of ways.

You must learn information that is "widely known" in your field. You will learn which ideas are common as you continue to study. If you aren't sure whether an idea is widely known or not, you should probably reference the information to be certain to avoid plagiarism.

Writing about a specific idea without providing a reference to explain its origins is considered plagiarism. Specific ideas are usually: an author's unique idea, the results of specific research or a statistic.

> Example: Research that has been done by Dr. Oz suggests that patients who listen to calming music and use meditation before surgery recover faster than patients who don't (Oz, 2003).

This requires a reference because it discusses the results of specific research.

References

Here are some basic citation formats with examples of how to reference source material according to APA style. Your sources should be listed in alphabetical order, according to the authors' last names.

REFERENCING A BOOK	
Last name, First Initial., & Last name, First Initial. (Year). *Book title: Subtitle*. (Edition) [if other than the 1st]. Place: Publisher.	Davis-Floyd, R., & St. John, G. (1998). *From doctor to healer: The transformative journey*. New Brunswick, NJ: Rutgers University Press.

REFERENCING A CHAPTER IN A BOOK WITH AN EDITOR	
Essay Author's Last name, First Initial. (Year). Essay title. In Editor's First Initial. Last Name (Ed.), *Book title* (pp. #–#). Place: Publisher.	Tauber, A.I. (1995). From the self to the other: Building a philosophy of medicine. In M.A. Grodin (Ed.), *Meta medical ethics: The philosophical foundations of bioethics* (pp. 158–95). Dordrecht, The Netherlands: Kluwer.

REFERENCING AN ACADEMIC JOURNAL OR A MAGAZINE *WITHOUT* A DIGITAL OBJECT IDENTIFIER (DOI)	
Last name, First Initial. (Year, Month Day). Article title. *Journal/ Magazine Title*. *Volume*/Issue number, page numbers [inclusive: the page numbers of the entire article].	Engel, G.L. (1977, April 8). The need for a new medical model: A challenge for biomedicine. *Science, 196*, 129–136.

REFERENCING AN ACADEMIC JOURNAL *WITH* A DIGITAL OBJECT IDENTIFIER (DOI)	
Last name, First Initial. (Year, Month Day). Article title. *Journal/ Magazine Title*. *Volume*/Issue number, page numbers. doi	Ernst, E., & Posadzki, P. (2011, December 15). Complementary and alternative medicine for rheumatoid arthritis and osteoarthritis: An overview of systematic reviews. *Current Pain and Headache Reports, 15*(6), 431–437. doi: 10.1007/s11916-011-0227-x

REFERENCING A NEWSPAPER	
Author's Last Name, First Initial. (Year, Month Day). Article title. *Newspaper Title*, page numbers.	Schwartz, J. (1993, September 30). Obesity affects economic, social status. *Washington Post*, pp. A1, A4.

REFERENCING A NEWSPAPER CONSULTED ONLINE	
Author's Last Name, First Initial. (Year, Month Day). Article title. *Newspaper Title*. Retrieved from: URL of article's homepage	Picard, A. (2011, October 31). We need a health care plan for boomers now. *Globe and Mail*. Retrieved from: http://www.theglobeandmail.com

A. With a classmate, write a reference for each of the following:

1 This book or another book that you have with you

_____

_____

_____

_____

2 A newspaper article that your teacher has brought to class or one that you can find online

_____

_____

_____

_____

3 A magazine or academic journal article that your teacher has brought to class or one that you can find online

_____

_____

_____

_____

B. When you have finished, your teacher may ask you to write your reference(s) on the board. Compare your references with those of other students. Remember to use accurate punctuation.

FINAL ASSIGNMENT
Write a Longer Compare and Contrast Essay

Write a compare and contrast essay to explain the similarities and differences between two models of medicine. Choose between

• the biomedical model of medicine and one of the systems of CAM from Reading 2;

• the humanistic model of medicine and one of the systems of CAM from Reading 2.

Use academic perspective in your essay. Quote and refer to information from the chapter readings, using appropriate in-text citations and references. Refer to the Models Chapter (page 187) to see an example of a compare and contrast essay and to learn more about how to write one.

CHAPTER 6

Vaccines

Most of us have experienced the prick of a needle at some point in our lives. Although we may not like the experience, we usually allow doctors or nurses to vaccinate us because we believe that the injection will help us resist a certain disease. However, vaccination has always been controversial, and there are people all over the world who refuse to be vaccinated or to have their children vaccinated. In many countries, the anti-vaccination movement is strong, and vaccine "risk-awareness" organizations host websites that have persuasive anti-vaccination messages.

How can we evaluate information both *for* and *against* vaccination to determine whether or not we should be vaccinated?

In this chapter, you will

- learn vocabulary related to the immune system and vaccination;

- learn how to paraphrase to avoid plagiarism;
- paraphrase a paragraph;
- learn about problems with writing in the third-person academic perspective, and how to avoid them;

- learn to consider the reliability of online information for evaluation purposes;
- write a process essay that includes a paraphrase.

GEARING UP

A. Working in a group of three, write your names at the top of the columns in the table. Discuss your answers to the questions, and write brief notes about your classmates' responses in the columns under their names.

	_____	_____	_____
Were you vaccinated when you were a child? Why or why not?			
When you travel, do you get vaccinations for your destination country? Why or why not?			
Do you get a vaccine to protect against the flu every year? Why or why not?			
Have you ever had an adverse (negative) reaction to a vaccine? If so, what happened?			

B. Are there differences of opinion or experience among your group members? If so, what are the differences? Report the results of your discussion to your classmates. Take a count of those students who are *for* and who are *against* vaccination.

The Body's Defenses

When we speak or write in English about vaccination programs and diseases, we often use words that relate to war. We compare the battle against disease to fighting a battle of war.

This similarity between fighting a disease and fighting a war is an *analogy*: a way of showing how different things are similar. If you are aware of this analogy, you will be able to select appropriate vocabulary when you speak or write about the topic.

A. Study the military words and their definitions. When you have finished, work with a partner and quiz each other on the meanings.

MILITARY OR WAR-RELATED WORDS	DEFINITION
defense (n.)	act of protecting against an attack
defense mechanisms* (n.)	reactions or responses that protect
disposal system (n.)	process designed to eliminate something dangerous
dispose* (v.) of	get rid of or destroy
eliminate* (v.) the threat	defeat or kill someone to prevent them from causing trouble
external* defenses (n.)	outside defenses designed to protect
hostile agent (n.)	spy who works for an opposing government or police department to gather secret information
internal criminals (n.)	people on the inside of an organization (or government) who are involved in illegal activities
invader (n.)	soldier or group of soldiers who enter a town and take control of it
optimal resistance (n.)	best way to fight against an attack
penetrate (v.) the defenses	enter and pass through, especially when this is difficult
trained observers (n.)	people who regularly watch and report on actions and events
weapons (n.) to knock out	items used to fight others with (e.g., gun)

* Appears on the Academic Word List

B. Read the following excerpt from a biology textbook and underline the military terms used to draw the analogy. This will allow you to see how these words and expressions are used in a biology context.

C. When you have identified all the words, answer the questions that follow the reading.

How the Immune System Works

The problem of defense against a pathogen is fairly analogous to that faced by a country at war or fighting its own internal criminals—namely, how to avoid damage by hostile agents—and in fact

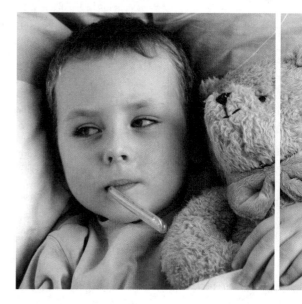

5 the solutions arrived at by nature and by governments are remarkably similar, so the often-used "war/police" analogies, though they are only analogies, will be
10 used quite often …

Nature's method operates at three levels:

1. To keep pathogens out by setting up effective *external defenses*;

15 2. If pathogens get in, catch and dispose of them rapidly, using an always ready and available army of cells and molecules: the *innate immune system*;

20 3. If this fails, devote a specialized set of cells to each pathogen, able to identify it, mark it for disposal and retain memory of its details for the future: the *adaptive immune system*.

External Defenses

These are the easiest defense mechanisms to understand, corresponding roughly to
25 the various strategies a medieval city might use for defense: thick walls (skin), arrow slits (eyelashes), pots of boiling oil (mucus), etc.

The Immune System

This term covers the complex network of organs, cells and molecules scattered throughout the body, whose function is to deal with infectious organisms that pen-
30 etrate the external defenses. They fall into two broad categories: *innate* and *adaptive*. To work properly, an immune system requires three sets of components:

1. A *recognition* system to identify the presence of the invader: this is carried out at the molecular level by various recognition molecules;

2. A *disposal* system to kill or otherwise eliminate the threat from the invader: disposal
35 is carried out at both molecular and cellular levels;

3. A *communication* system to coordinate the activities of the various recognition and disposal elements and to limit damage to the host and return the system to its previous condition (homeostasis).

As already hinted, this is very much the way a country defends itself against enemy
40 agents: 1) trained observers identify them, 2) weapons knock them out, and 3) radio
keeps everyone in touch. And in a very similar way to an army, all these immune
components are characterized by a high degree of *mobility*, a feature unique to the
immune system. This makes sense, considering that it is impossible to know in
advance where the invader will choose to attack …

45 ## Innate and Adaptive Immunity

The immune system divides conveniently into two parts—the *innate* and the *adaptive*
immune systems—which differ in a number of important ways. A comparison
(Table 9.5) shows that with innate immunity the emphasis is on disposal, while recognition is comparatively broad in its specificity. On the other hand, adaptive immu-
50 nity, which evolved much more recently, features an extremely high degree of
specificity of recognition, different for individual cells, while adding relatively less in
the way of new disposal mechanisms, often leaving this task to the innate system …

**Table 9.5: The division of the immune system into innate and adaptive components
is based on several important differences**

	INNATE IMMUNITY	ADAPTIVE IMMUNITY
EVOLUTIONARY ORIGIN	Earliest animals, all invertebrates and vertebrates	Vertebrates only
PRINCIPAL CELLS	Phagocytes	Lymphocytes
PRINCIPAL MOLECULES	Complement, cytokines	Antibody, cytokines
SPECIFICITY OF RECOGNITION	Broad	Very high specificity*
SPEED OF ACTION	Rapid (minutes, hours)	Slow (days)
DEVELOPMENT OF MEMORY	No	Yes*

* High specificity and memory are the hallmarks of adaptive immunity.

Evolution and the Time Element

Two other important differences between innate and adaptive immune processes have
55 to do with the *time* factor. The innate system has evolved extremely slowly, from species to species over hundreds of millions of years,
but when it goes into action, it does so very rapidly.
In contrast, the adaptive immune system is evolu-
tionarily recent (dating from the earliest verte-
60 brates) while its recognition molecules complete
their evolution in a matter of days, within the life-
times of each individual animal; however, its
responses, because they involve an element of cell
proliferation, tend to be slower to take effect. To
65 take two examples, the activation of complement
and of phagocytosis by macrophages (innate),
occur within minutes, while the production of antibody (adaptive), which requires two different kinds

of lymphocyte and several cycles of cell division, can take a week or more. Fortunately
70 lymphocyte responses display *memory,* ensuring that a subsequent response to the
same pathogen occurs much faster. Thus the adaptive immune response is more flexible and vigorous, so much so that it requires quite sophisticated *regulatory* mechanisms
to stop it going on too long or causing damage to its possessor …

Since higher animals possess both innate and adaptive immune systems, it was always
75 assumed, very reasonably, that both systems are important for optimal resistance to
infection. But the degree to which they are interactive and interdependent has only
been appreciated recently.

Playfair, J., & Bancroft, G. (2008). *Infection and immunity* (3rd ed., pp. 64–75). Oxford, UK: Oxford University Press.

1 What are the body's three systems of defense?

_____

_____

2 Give examples of the first defense system.

_____

_____

3 What are the three requirements for an effective immune system?

_____

_____

4 What are the important differences between the innate and adaptive immune systems?

_____

_____

5 What fact about the body's immune systems was recently discovered and was surprising?

_____

_____

VOCABULARY BUILD

A. Working with a partner, look at how the words in bold are used in the following sentences. For each, write the part of speech in the parentheses: *n.* for noun; *v.* for verb; *adj.* for adjective. The first one has been done for you. When you have finished, check with other students to be sure that you understand the meaning of the words.

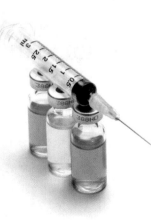

1 The doctor filled the **syringe** (___*n.*___) with the **vaccine** (___*n.*___).

2 The idea that **vaccination** (_____) might prevent disease began with an English doctor who noticed that once people had recovered from a disease, they did not **contract** (_____) the same disease again.

3 In order **to be vaccinated** (_____) against a disease, you must have a **needle** (_____).

4 The needle **injects** (_____) a milder and inactive form of the disease into your body.

5 Once the **inoculation** (_____) is complete, your body will develop **immunity** (_____) to the disease. In other words, it will **resist** (_____) the disease in the future.

6 The doctor **vaccinated** (_____) all the children; now the children are **immune** (_____) to that disease.

7 The **immunization** (_____) program had a goal of vaccinating 90 percent of people over the age of seventy-five against the **flu** (_____).

8 **Adverse** (_____) reactions to routine vaccinations are **rare** (_____).

B. Synonyms are words that have the same meaning. Using synonyms can add variety to your speaking and writing. It can also help you paraphrase (express in your own words) someone else's ideas. From this list of words, group the synonyms together. Pay attention to the forms of the words.

Example: immunize (v.), inoculate (v.), vaccinate (v.),

adverse (adj.)	get (v.)	*inoculate* (v.)	protected (adj.) against
contract* (v.)	immunization (n.)	inoculation (n.)	shot (n.)
eliminate* (v.)	*immunize* (v.)	knock out (v.)	syringe (n.)
elimination* (n.)	immune (adj.) from	needle (n.)	*vaccinate* (v.)
eradicate (v.)	inject (v.)	negative (adj.)	vaccination (n.)
eradication (n.)	injection (n.)		

* Appears on the Academic Word List

_____

_____

_____

_____

_____

_____

Academic
Survival Skill

Avoiding Plagiarism by Paraphrasing

As you now know, copying another person's words or ideas is called *plagiarism*, and it is considered an academic "crime." In Chapter 5, you learned why plagiarism is a serious concern and how you can avoid it by providing a reference for quoted information. You can also avoid plagiarism by paraphrasing. However, even if you choose to paraphrase another person's words or ideas, you will still need to provide an in-text citation and reference your source.

Although you may use quotations to express specific ideas, it is best to use your own words when writing your assignments. Expressing another person's words or ideas in your own words is called *paraphrasing*.

Characteristics of a good paraphrase:

• The paraphrase has the same meaning as the original writing.

• The paraphrase is roughly the same length as the original writing.

• The original words and structures of the source, except for technical words or very common words ("public domain" words), have been rephrased.

The following techniques will help you paraphrase successfully. Usually, you will use more than one technique to paraphrase well.

Use appropriate synonyms.

Examples:

syringe	⟶ needle	eliminate a disease	⟶	eradicate a disease
disease	⟶ sickness	develop immunity	⟶	acquire resistance
vaccination	⟶ immunization	immune from	⟶	protected against

Some words from the original text, such as the names of people, countries, religions, diseases and scientific terms, cannot be changed because they have no synonyms.

Change the sentence type.

To use this technique, you must ask yourself, "What is the sentence structure of the original writing?" Once you have answered this question, you can change the sentence structure to avoid plagiarism.

Original source (single independent clause)
The successful use of vaccines in preventing disease means most people in Canada today have never seen a life-threatening case of diphtheria, polio or even measles.

Change the sentence structure to independent clause + dependent clause.
Most people in Canada today have never seen a life-threatening case of diphtheria, polio or even measles because the use of vaccines in preventing disease has been successful.

Add appropriate synonyms to form a paraphrased sentence.
The majority of Canadians these days don't experience dangerous diseases like diphtheria, polio or measles as immunizations to eliminate sickness have worked.

Change the voice from active to passive—or from passive to active.

Original source (active voice)
Unfortunately, a small minority of people actively oppose immunization.

Change to passive voice.
Unfortunately, immunization is actively opposed by a small minority of people.

Add appropriate synonyms to form a paraphrased sentence.
It is disappointing that vaccination is rejected by a tiny segment of the population.

Change the parts of speech.

To use this technique, change nouns into verbs, adjectives into adverbs, verbs into adjectives, adjectives into nouns and so on.

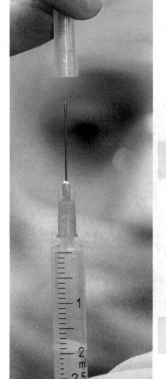

Original source

Vaccines (n.) strengthen (v.) the immune system to protect (v.) children and adults from specific diseases.

Change the parts of speech wherever possible.

Vaccination (n.) makes the immune system stronger (adj.) for the protection (n.) of children and adults against specific diseases.

Add appropriate synonyms.

Immunization creates a strong immune system in order to resist certain sicknesses that may harm people.

Change the sentence structure and voice (from active to passive).

A strong immune system that resists deadly diseases is created by immunization.

Quick tips to help you paraphrase successfully.

- You may need to use more than one technique to paraphrase successfully.
- You must understand the original writing before you try to paraphrase it.
- When you have finished your paraphrase, it must make sense.

A. With one or two classmates, paraphrase the following sentences in writing.

1 Vaccines are safe for almost everyone although, very rarely, there are people who experience adverse reactions.

_____

_____

2 Some mild side effects are experienced by most people after they are immunized.

_____

_____

B. Compare your answers with those of other students. Is one paraphrase better than another? Why or why not?

WARM-UP ASSIGNMENT
Paraphrase a Paragraph

Now that you have learned how to paraphrase, paraphrase *one* of the following two paragraphs, using the techniques you just learned.

Paragraph One

Vaccination—and especially mass childhood immunization—is acclaimed as the most successful and effective form of public health intervention that there has ever been. It has acquired a special character, symbolizing high hopes of lives saved, diseases eradicated and the power of medical technology in an apparent triumph of science over nature ... From the smallpox vaccination campaigns of nineteenth-century

Europe to the international community's growing investments in mass childhood immunization across the world, this technology offers a universal promise of disease control that can appear to trump national and local interests.

Paragraph Two

Vaccines link the most global with the most local and personal. Aiming to reach every child on the planet, vaccination technology has a uniquely global character. Vaccines are produced, distributed and monitored within systems that are equally globalized. Yet vaccination reaches from the global into the most intimate world of parenting and care. As a technology, it enters the intense social world in which parents and caregivers seek to help their children flourish, spanning genders and generations, comrades and communities and advice givers. These are everyday worlds that vary enormously across the globe, and over time.

Leach, M., & Fairhead, J. (2007). *Vaccine anxieties: Global science, child health and society* (pp. 1–2). London, UK: Earthscan.

VOCABULARY BUILD

A. Familiarize yourself with the names of diseases by matching the disease with its symptoms. Confirm your answers with the class. Are any of these diseases common in the country(ies) in which you live (have lived)? Are there other common diseases for which there are no vaccines?

DISEASE	SYMPTOMS
❶ diphtheria	_____ Causes coughing that is difficult to stop. Can be fatal.
❷ hepatitis B	_____ Causes fever, sore throat, runny nose and red spots on the body.
❸ influenza (flu)	_____ Causes painful swelling in the neck.
❹ measles	_____ Causes red spots on the body. Can damage an unborn child if the mother is infected.
❺ mumps	_____ Causes muscle degeneration ranging from twisted arms and legs to an interruption of breathing. Can be fatal.
❻ pertussis (whooping cough)	___1___ Causes infection of the throat that makes breathing difficult. Can be fatal.
❼ polio	_____ Occurs when bacteria penetrate the skin and causes the muscles, and especially the jaw, to become stiff.
❽ rabies	_____ Causes infection of various body parts, but especially the lungs. Makes breathing difficult. Can be fatal.
❾ rubella	_____ Occurs when bitten by an infected animal. Causes headache, fever, pain, violent movements. Can be fatal.
❿ smallpox	_____ Causes symptoms of a bad cold: runny nose, sore throat, aching muscles, sometimes fever.
⓫ tetanus (lock jaw)	_____ Causes red spots on the skin. Can be fatal. Has been eradicated worldwide.
⓬ tuberculosis (TB)	_____ Causes inflammation of the liver and vomiting. Can be fatal.

B. Work with a partner to define these key words from the reading. The words are presented in short example sentences to provide clues to their meaning. Confirm your answers with the class or a dictionary.

WORDS IN CONTEXT	DEFINITION
1 The **adaptive*** immune system can change over time to help the body resist attack by a virus.	adaptive: *able to change*
2 The immune system fights **pathogens** that can cause infection.	pathogens:
3 An **attenuated** strain of a disease is not as infectious as the pathogenic strain of the same disease.	attenuated:
4 To eradicate a disease, vaccines must be globally **available**.*	available:
5 To be **beneficial**,* a vaccine must first be safe to use.	beneficial:
6 BCG are the letters that **correspond*** to the tuberculosis vaccine.	correspond:
7 There are four **criteria*** that a vaccine must meet before it is implemented.	criteria:
8 When people are inoculated, their immune systems are **enhanced**.*	enhanced:
9 It can be **enormously*** expensive to develop and distribute a new vaccine.	enormously:
10 The World Health Organization (WHO) **estimates*** that three million lives are saved by vaccines every year.	estimates:

▶

WORDS IN CONTEXT	DEFINITION
⑪ The **function*** of a vaccine is to build up the adaptive immune system without causing the disease.	function:
⑫ This **generation*** of children will never know smallpox.	generation:
⑬ Immunization **induces*** the body to produce antibodies that fight infection.	induces:
⑭ For vaccines made from live viruses, it is essential they be kept cold. During transportation, the "cold chain" must be **maintained**.*	maintained:
⑮ The adaptive immune system has **specific*** memory for a pathogen.	specific:
⑯ If people are **susceptible** to a disease, they must be very careful to protect themselves from infection.	susceptible:
⑰ Very infectious diseases have high rates of **transmission**.* They spread from person to person rapidly.	transmission:

* Appears on the Academic Word List

READING ② Control of Infectious Disease

This reading has been taken from a biology textbook. Read the excerpt and then answer the questions that follow.

Vaccination

Immunization makes use of the ability of the adaptive immune system to learn and improve. It may be active, inducing the immune system itself to acquire a permanently enhanced resistance to a particular pathogen, or passive, where preformed antibody
5 is introduced into the individual to be protected. Active immunization directed at a specific organism is known as *vaccination*, in commemoration of Edward Jenner's pioneering work (1797) on the prevention of smallpox by scarification with vaccinia (cowpox). Smallpox has now been eradicated (1980) but ever since Pasteur showed in the 1880s that it was possible to immunize against other infections, the general term
10 *vaccination* has been retained.

The function of a vaccine is to induce memory without causing disease, so that the pathogen itself, on first contact with the patient, provokes a secondary rather than a primary response, and a response of the right kind to be effective ...

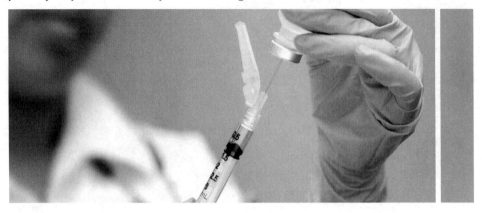

Requirements for a Vaccine

15 There are not vaccines for every disease; this is because a vaccine, to be worth bringing into use, must satisfy four criteria. It must be 1) effective, 2) safe, 3) stable and 4) affordable.

Effectiveness

The best vaccines are very effective indeed. As mentioned above, Jenner's cowpox
20 vaccine eventually eliminated smallpox, and several other viral diseases have been targeted by the World Health Organization (WHO) for eradication within the next generation; these include measles, rubella, mumps and polio. Whether or not this is achieved, there is no doubt that in the developed world, these four diseases are disappearing rapidly, and the same is true for the "toxic" bacterial diseases tetanus and
25 diphtheria. It is estimated that vaccination currently saves some three million lives per year, a figure that could increase to five million if vaccines were available universally.

At the other end of the scale, there are vaccines that, although undoubtedly beneficial, stand no chance at present of eradicating the corresponding disease; examples are influenza, rabies and BCG (the tuberculosis vaccine).

30 Note that it may not always be necessary to vaccinate every single member of the population for two reasons: 1) when most individuals are protected and few are susceptible, transmission becomes increasingly difficult and the disease may eventually die out (so-called *herd immunity*); 2) an attenuated strain may actually replace the pathogenic type in the environment, as is happening with live polio vaccine in
35 water supplies, so that individuals become immunized without knowing it.

The reasons for reduced effectiveness differ. In the case of influenza, antigenic variation makes it hard to match the vaccine to the current virus strain. With rabies, there is a large wild animal population beyond the reach of the vaccinator. With BCG, the problem is that it works much better in some parts of the world than others, for
40 reasons that are not fully understood but probably reflect the influence of other bacteria in the local environment as well as genetic differences between human populations. However, the use of BCG is so universal that it would be ethically and politically difficult to replace it experimentally with an alternative ...

Finally, there are diseases for which no
45 vaccine is currently available at all:
leading examples are the common
cold, staphylococcal infections and vir-
tually all fungal, protozoal and worm
infections. The reason is usually tech-
50 nical, but may also be economic …

Safety

Safety is an increasingly critical consideration. One must remember that vaccines are the only medical treatment
55 administered to perfectly healthy
people, and "vaccine accidents"—real
or imaginary—can lead to public alarm
and enormously expensive litigation …
Partly for these reasons, and partly

60 because of the low profitability of vaccines compared to chemotherapy (using chemicals to attack microbes), many pharmaceutical companies nowadays are cautious of
new vaccine development.

Stability

Stability becomes particularly important where vaccines are used far from their site
65 of manufacture, and is again chiefly a problem for living vaccines, where maintenance
of the "cold chain" between producer and consumer requires careful monitoring at
all stages of the journey.

Affordability

Most vaccines are remarkably cheap; indeed, vaccination has been called the most cost-
70 effective form of preventative medicine ever invented. For example, the cost of vaccinating a child against measles, pertussis, diphtheria, tetanus, polio and TB is less than
US $20. However, it must be borne in mind that for some tropical countries, even a few
cents per person per year may exceed the available health budget. Moreover, some vaccines are definitely not cheap: the hepatitis B vaccine still costs around $60 per individual,
75 having fallen from $125! To introduce a *new* vaccine is extremely expensive.

Playfair, J., & Bancroft, G. (2008). *Infection and immunity* (3rd ed., pp. 244–249). Oxford, UK: Oxford University
Press.

1 What is the function of a vaccine?

_____

_____

2 What are the four requirements for a successful vaccine?

_____

_____

▶

3 What proof is there that vaccines are effective?

_____

_____

_____

_____

4 In what two ways may individuals be protected from a disease even without immunization?

_____

_____

_____

_____

5 Why may vaccines have reduced effectiveness?

_____

_____

6 How do high safety standards make it difficult for pharmaceutical companies to develop vaccines?

_____

_____

_____

7 What is the "cold chain"?

_____

_____

8 Are vaccines expensive or cheap? Explain your answer.

_____

_____

FOCUS ON WRITING

Writing in the Third Person

Most academic writing is completed in the third person and in the present tense because

- academic writing should have an academic perspective (third person) to show objectivity (see Chapter 5, page 100); and
- academic writing discusses facts or repeated actions (present tense).

Writers may choose to use the third-person _singular_ perspective (_he, she, it, everybody, anyone, nothing_) or the third-person _plural_ perspective (_they_) in the present tense.

If you use the third-person singular perspective, you may have problems with a) subject-verb agreement in the present tense and b) pronoun-antecedent agreement.

Subject-verb agreement in the present tense

Remember to add _-s_ or _-es_ to a present-tense verb to agree with a third-person singular subject. Subject-verb agreement must also be respected in relative clauses.

PROBLEM: Often students forget to make verbs agree with third-person singular subjects.

SOLUTION: Switch to a third-person plural perspective.

SINGULAR SUBJECT/PRESENT TENSE	PLURAL SUBJECT/PRESENT TENSE
A *vaccine works* by allowing the body to develop immunity to a disease before the *disease strikes*.	*Vaccines work* by allowing the body to develop immunity to diseases before the *diseases strike*.
Fear of possible adverse reactions *convinces* some parents not to vaccinate their children.	*Fears* of possible adverse reactions *convince* some parents not to vaccinate their children.
Extensive media coverage, which *increases* awareness of adverse reactions to vaccines, often *does not reflect* the real likelihood of an adverse reaction occurring.	*Extensive media reports,* which *increase* awareness of adverse reactions to vaccines, often *do not reflect* the real likelihood of an adverse reaction occurring. (There is no plural form of *media coverage*.)
Parents want all possible *information* that *relates* to vaccine safety.	Parents want all possible statistics that *relate* to vaccine safety. (There is no plural form of *information*.)

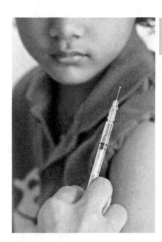

Pronoun-antecedent agreement with the third-person singular

Remember to make your pronouns agree in number and gender with the antecedent (the corresponding noun).

PROBLEM: Using singular pronouns can be awkward, or can exclude either males or females.

SOLUTION: Switch to a third-person plural perspective.

SINGULAR SUBJECT/PRESENT TENSE	PLURAL SUBJECT/PRESENT TENSE
A *parent* may think *his or her* child's risk of experiencing an adverse reaction is low as *his or her* child is healthy and *he or she* is well-informed about vaccine safety. (Problem: is awkward)	*Parents* may think *their* child's risk of experiencing an adverse reaction is low as *their* child is healthy and *they* are well-informed about vaccine safety.
A *child* may find *his* skin becomes red and itchy, or *his* arm may be sore at the injection site. (Problem: excludes female children)	*Children* may find *their* skin becomes red and itchy, or *their* arms may be sore at the injection site.

Of course, it isn't always possible to switch to a third-person plural subject. In this case, you can look specifically for these errors (subject-verb agreement and pronoun-antecedent agreement) once a draft of the writing is complete.

On the next page, there are five incorrectly written sentences. Revise these sentences to eliminate problems that occur when writing in the third-person *singular* perspective. Shift these sentences into the third-person *plural* perspective.

It may be helpful to proofread sentence by sentence, from the bottom of the writing to the top, so that you can focus on grammatical correctness instead of information presentation.

1 A newborn infant should be vaccinated to avoid the possibility that she may contract a disease early in her life.

_____

_____

2 An unvaccinated child that live long enough to be exposed to a disease can contract that disease.

_____

_____

3 A vaccine that reduce the chance of death is beneficial to society.

_____

_____

4 Sometimes, a person can't be vaccinated. He or she may have a severe allergic reaction to some part of the vaccine, or his or her immune system may be too weak to receive the vaccine.

_____

_____

_____

5 A tourist who accidentally expose himself to a disease may bring his sickness back to his country.

_____

_____

READING ③ Vaccine Brain Damage

A. This reading is the story of a person who claims she suffered brain damage due to hepatitis B vaccination. The story comes from the Vaccine Risk Awareness Network (VRAN), which is an anti-vaccine website. Skim the first few paragraphs and discuss some of the differences between this autobiographical narrative and Readings 1 and 2, which came from biology textbooks.

B. Read the story and then answer the questions that follow.

Aftermath of Hepatitis B Shots by Lucia Morgan

It's been nearly three years since I became chronically ill. I can tell you the day and the hour it began. It was shortly after I received my second hepatitis B shot. I had recently completed a master's degree. Six months after the shot, I could barely read.

5 I had trouble following TV shows. I missed puns and couldn't pick up on social cues. Anything but a few minutes of a simple conversation left me hopelessly confused.

Before this, my lifestyle was active and varied. I worked full-time, renovated my home, swam, canoed, practised tai chi and did black-and-white photography. Now I could barely look after myself. My morning shower left me exhausted. It was all I could do
10 to make my own meals. My sleep was so shallow, I didn't know if I was thinking or

dreaming: when I was awake I felt barely conscious. I couldn't drive or go to a movie, let alone work. I was plagued with joint pain, fevers, intense
15 chills, intestinal problems, constant exhaustion and difficulty speaking. At times I thought I was dying.

I developed flu symptoms immediately after my first shot. This should have been
20 a warning, but I had started a new job and assumed I was run down from stress. I should have been tested at this time to see whether I had "sero-converted" (developed resistance to hepatitis B).
25 Failure to sero-convert indicates that fur- ther vaccination is dangerous (three shots are necessary to complete the series). My condition may have been much milder if I'd known to request testing. (It is possible to pre-test an individual prior to receiving serum from a bad batch, but it can
30 certainly reduce risks.)

The extensive fatigue I experienced does not result from lack of conditioning as my insurance company would like to think. Exhaustion comes from certain areas of the brain being overloaded; to compensate for the damage, they have taken over func- tions they weren't designed to perform. When overworked, they start to shut down.
35 It is nearly impossible to keep going.

In the first year of my recovery, neural pathways were rerouted; this accounts for some of my initial progress. Acupuncture, a yeast-free diet, oil of evening primrose and an individualized vitamin regimen all helped me make further gains. But now, three years later, only minimal improvement is probable. I do learn more ways to
40 maximize my energy as time goes by, but the brain damage I have is irreversible. And pushing myself past my limits only worsens the condition.

Starting Over

My physician diagnosed chronic fatigue syndrome. Three months later he found me a specialist whose focus was nutrition, vitamin supplements and strengthening the
45 immune system. With much persistence, I obtained long-term disability benefits and was able to stay in my tiny, manageable one-bedroom house. My children were grown. I was in a supportive relationship, and most people did not question my diagnosis.

I made slow but steady recovery for a year, then plateaued. My doctors were missing an important factor: the impact of the hepatitis shots. They thought it was merely a
50 trigger: "the straw that broke the camel's back."

My chiropractor saw it differently. Her profession has heightened concern regarding vaccinations. After much searching, she put me in touch with the Nightingale Foun- dation in Ottawa where Dr. Byron Hyde was researching cases of CFS induced by hepatitis shots. I am not an isolated case though health authorities would have you
55 believe otherwise.

Problems with hepatitis shots have been noted in Canada since at least 1990. Over fifty health-care workers in Hull, Quebec had acute reactions, forcing them to leave work, many never to fully recover. One went deaf, another blind, and a third fell into a coma and died. It took me many months to make contact with the founda-
60 tion and obtain an appointment. The government has continually refused to fund this research, and resources are extremely limited. Out of 1,000 people that present themselves yearly, only thirty or forty can be taken on as patients. And it is not as if the evidence of suffering or damage is unclear or obscure. It can be established by a properly administered brain SPECT scan.

65 It was this scan that provided me with the most crushing of diagnoses since becoming ill: permanent brain damage. In my case, when I received the inocula-tions, my body formed no antibodies. Instead, the substance attacked my central nervous system. I was asked if I'd ever had electroshock treatments. Apparently my brain scan showed this type of damage. Today I am somewhat better. I can read
70 simple novels, go for short walks, do a bit of writing and some of my own house-work. I still have bad headaches, frequent flu symptoms, persistent fatigue and find that physical exertion greatly depletes my intellectual capacity. My energy level is probably one-eighth of what it was when I was well.

Targeted Teens

75 It is hard for me to imagine what it must be like for the grade seven Ontario students inoculated over the last four years! If they became as ill as I did, then their futures would be greatly compromised. I wonder how many of them are being accused of using drugs, or being lazy and unmotivated, when they are in fact suffering the rav-ages of hepatitis shots?

80 Though a 1986 Ontario law requires that patients be informed of the vaccine's dangers beforehand, the student consent form states only that the hepatitis vaccine might cause mild side effects such as slight fever, sore arm and tiredness for a day or so. They do not mention brain damage, loss of faculties or death. Nor do they warn that the vaccine can trigger any of the multiple viruses in our systems that we fight off
85 every minute of the day.

I feel grave concern for all those young students who are vulnerable to the damage I have suffered. And for them, the ravages will be far worse.

I am able to write this article because my learning was not arrested in adolescence. This is when much of our social and intellectual development takes place. Though I am
90 slow to process information and can write only for short stints, I know how to problem-solve, to set and pursue long-term goals and have the self-esteem to take risks. I've learned these skills from experiencing the normal successes and stresses of adult life. At grade seven, children have barely begun to develop these capacities.

By starting at a high level of functioning, I have paid a price. Testing arranged by my
95 insurance company has found me "cognitively and psychologically fit for daily living and full-time employment." The fact I am so physically impaired that I can barely take care of my daily living needs, let alone work, has been flagrantly disregarded.

My long-term disability benefits are now in dispute. I may be forced to apply for welfare and am in danger of losing my home. Knowing what I know now, I would never have had the inoculations. They have narrowed my potential, my future, my life. In the meantime, I try to make the best of my situation and warn others of the danger.

100

Morgan, L. (2002, October 1). Vaccine brain damage: Aftermath of hepatitis B shots. Retrieved from: http://vran.org/personal-stories/vaccine-brain-damage/

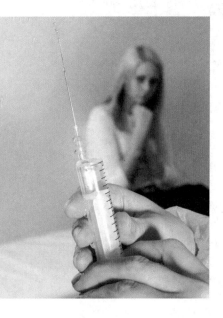

1 In point form, and in chronological order, retell the events of Lucia's story.

_____

_____

_____

_____

_____

_____

_____

_____

_____

_____

_____

_____

_____

_____

2 Do you believe Lucia's brain damage was caused by the hepatitis B vaccine? Why or why not?

_____

_____

_____

3 Does Lucia have scientific proof to demonstrate that her brain damage was caused by the vaccine? Explain your answer.

_____

_____

_____

C. When you have completed the questions, compare your answers with those of another student. Do you believe that vaccination is safe? Why or why not?

Evaluating Information

In your search for information about vaccines, you will probably come across sources you're not sure about. The questions below will help you judge whether or not the information is reliable. These questions were written specifically for information obtained from the Internet but they are useful to ask of any media source, including newspapers, magazines, radio, tabloids, pamphlets or books.

What is the source of the information?
• The website should clearly identify the person or organization that produced it.
• The site should provide a way to contact the provider of the information.

Has the medical information been reviewed by scientific experts?
• If so, the experts should be identified, including their credentials (degrees, positions, etc.).

Is there a date indicating when the information was last revised?
• If so, is it current?

Is there scientific evidence to support the claims?
• If so, the site should provide sources (e.g., articles from medical journals) for the scientific evidence (e.g., studies, reports, statistics).

Is the site certified by the Health On the Net Foundation?
• The Health On the Net (HON) Foundation is a Swiss not-for-profit organization working to help Internet users find useful and reliable online medical information. HON has developed a set of guidelines for health sites. Sites that meet the criteria can use the HON seal to show they follow the code of conduct. The HON site (www.hon.ch) also has a checklist to help users judge whether a given site would meet the criteria.

Anti-Vaccination Websites

A study[1] of twenty-two websites that oppose vaccination found that the sites shared a number of features:
• They made the same false claims about vaccines.
• They all had links to other anti-vaccination sites.
• Many promoted alternative systems of health care—such as homeopathy, naturopathy and chiropractic—as being superior to vaccination.
• More than half provided anecdotes about children who had allegedly been damaged by vaccines.

False claims made on anti-vaccination websites include the following:
• Vaccines cause illnesses whose causes are unknown, such as autism (from MMR and/or DTaP), SIDS, immune dysfunction, diabetes, seizures, brain damage, attention deficit disorder, antisocial behaviour, asthma, allergy (100 percent of sites).
• Vaccines erode immunity or harm the immune system (95 percent of sites).
• Vaccine producers or government regulators are responsible for an under-reporting of adverse reactions because they cover up the truth about such events (95 percent of sites).

▶

1. Wolfe, F., Sharpe, L., & Lipsky, M. (2002, June 26). Content and design attributes of anti-vaccination websites. *Journal of American Medical Association, 287* (24), pp. 3245–8. doi: 10.1001/jama287.24.3245

- Vaccine policy is motivated by profit: manufacturers make enormous profits on vaccines, which influences vaccine recommendations and promotes cover-up of reactions (91 percent of sites).
- Vaccines are ineffective or produce only temporary immunity (82 percent of sites).
- Compulsory vaccination violates civil rights (77 percent of sites).
- Rates of disease declined prior to the use of vaccines due to improved nutrition (73 percent of sites).
- Lots of vaccines cause severe reactions (55 percent of sites).
- There is an increased risk of reactions from multiple simultaneous vaccines (50 percent of sites).
- Homeopathy, naturopathy, alternative medicine and breastfeeding enhance immunity better than vaccines.

If you are in doubt about any information you read or hear, discuss it with your health-care professional.

Determine how many of these characteristics are demonstrated in "Aftermath of Hepatitis B Shots." How do you evaluate this story?

_____

_____

_____

_____

_____

FINAL ASSIGNMENT
Write a Process Essay

Write a process essay, using the academic perspective, that answers the following question:

How do vaccines stimulate the adaptive immune system, and how can people evaluate information about vaccine safety?

In your essay introduction, include the paraphrase you wrote in the Warm-Up Assignment. Be sure to provide a citation of the original work and include the full reference in your references or bibliography.

Refer to the Models Chapter (page 183) to see an example of a process essay and to learn more about how to write one.

CHAPTER 7

Risk Perception

Are you safe? Do you expose yourself to unnecessary risks? Are you willing to travel to a city where there is an outbreak of a serious disease? Are you willing to climb a mountain, fly in an airplane or drive a car?

It is natural to fear risks; fearing risks allows you to avoid life-threatening situations. Your tolerance of risks is based on universal risk-response patterns. These patterns of response explain why your perception of risk may not match the facts.

GEARING UP

A. Working in a group of four, list those activities that you take part in every day that could be considered risky or dangerous. When the list is complete, put a check mark in the appropriate column to indicate whether the activity is *avoidable* or *unavoidable*.

ACTIVITIES THAT INVOLVE RISK	AVOIDABLE	UNAVOIDABLE
	☐	☐
	☐	☐
	☐	☐
	☐	☐
	☐	☐
	☐	☐
	☐	☐
	☐	☐
	☐	☐
	☐	☐
	☐	☐
	☐	☐

B. Discuss your list with the teacher and your classmates. What are the most risky or dangerous activities that you participate in? Why do you participate in these activities? Are there activities that you can't avoid, or that you could modify to reduce the risk?

A. The expressions in bold in the following sentences are often used when people talk about risk. With a partner, read the sentences and discuss what these expressions might mean. Check your ideas with the class, and write the meaning below the sentences.

1 When people **have control over** an activity such as driving, they often don't see their behaviour as **risky**.

MEANING: _____

_____

2 People are often more worried about a risk than they need to be. Their **risk perception*** is not supported by statistical data.

MEANING: _____

_____

3 Some people have a higher **risk tolerance** than others. For example, some people love to climb mountains, while others are afraid to travel by plane.

MEANING: _____

_____

_____

4 He thought he could do anything he wanted and not get hurt. He didn't understand the **consequences*** **of** his behaviour.

MEANING: _____

_____

_____

5 Dangerous chemicals can be a **hazard** in a laboratory setting.

MEANING: _____

_____

6 The **exposure*** **to** second-hand smoke can increase your chances of **contracting*** cancer.

MEANING: _____

_____

_____

7 Some people are so **cautious** that they avoid every activity—even activities that are not likely to cause them **harm**.

MEANING: _____

_____

_____

* Appears on the Academic Word List

B. Read the following text and then answer the questions. When you have finished, share your answers with the class.

Public Risk Perception

The auditorium was jammed. The TV cameras were lined up down in front, aimed back at the crowd, ready to roll at the first loud voice. The moderator opened the floor to comments. Susan Napolitano leaped to her feet, her eyes wide and her face red.

5 "That school could give our children cancer! We demand that you close it and clean it up before our children have to go back there!" she screamed at the officials sitting at the head table. Stabbing her finger at them, she yelled, "You are not our children's parents! You will not decide whether they live or die!"

Sitting next to her, Susan's ten-year-old daughter Stephie, looked up at her mom, a
10 little embarrassed at, and a little proud of, her mother's public display of passion on her behalf. Stephie was a student at a public elementary school … where trace amounts of the chemical trichloroethylene (TCE) had been found in the air of the library and one
15 third-grade classroom. TCE is a confirmed carcinogen (cancer-causing agent), but at the low levels found in the school, just a few molecules of TCE per trillion
20 molecules of air, even the most aggressive public health experts said that there was no threat. The TCE levels were well within safety standards. There was no danger.

25 But that didn't matter to Susan. As reporters flocked around her after the meeting, she told them that she was convinced Stephie could get cancer if she attended
30 the school, and she was willing to do anything necessary to get the school closed, even though that might mean taking kids who mostly walked to school and
35 busing them to other classrooms around town, on sometimes icy winter streets, disrupting their education and spending tens of thousands of dollars from the school department's already tight budget to institute those changes. All to eliminate a risk that, according to the scientific evidence, wasn't a risk at all.

40 Susan stood there in front of the TV cameras and reporters, flushed with passion, with Stephie at her side. And as she talked about her fear of those trace amounts of TCE, she anxiously puffed away on her tenth cigarette of the night. And mother and daughter were also taking another big risk: both were significantly overweight.

Ropeik, D. (2010). *How risky is it, really? Why our fears don't always match the facts* (pp. xi–xii). New York, NY: McGraw Hill.

1 What risk was Susan Napolitano worried about?

_____

_____

2 Why did Susan have a low tolerance for this risk?

_____

_____

3 What risks does Susan not seem to be worried about?

_____

_____

4 What is your opinion about Susan's tolerance for the various risks she and her daughter were exposed to?

_____

_____

FOCUS ON WRITING

Writing Conditional Sentences

Conditional sentences are useful when you want to discuss risk. They include an *if-clause* and a *main clause*. The likelihood of the outcome in the main clause depends on the condition expressed in the if-clause.

IF-CLAUSE (CONDITION)	MAIN CLAUSE (OUTCOME)
If people are familiar with a risk,	they will be less afraid of it.

There are three types of conditional sentences.

A possibility in the present or future

These sentences show that the condition is possible.

IF + PRESENT TENSE	WILL + SIMPLE FORM
If you expose yourself to the sun,	your skin will burn.
	CAN + SIMPLE FORM
If travellers are exposed to an infectious disease,	they can unknowingly transmit the disease to others when they return home.

Unlikely present or future

These sentences show that the condition is unlikely.

IF + PAST TENSE	WOULD + SIMPLE FORM
If you thought about the consequences of your actions,	you would not behave in this manner.
	COULD + SIMPLE FORM
If you drove through a red light,	you could be in an accident.

Impossible past

These sentences show that the condition is impossible because the time for action has already passed.

IF + PAST PERFECT TENSE	WOULD HAVE + PAST PARTICIPLE
If doctors had known how dangerous the SARS virus was,	they would have acted faster to contain it.
	COULD HAVE + PAST PARTICIPLE
If scientists had predicted the floods sooner,	many people could have escaped death.

Complete the following sentences by writing a main clause to match the if-clause.

1. If our children are at risk, _____

   _____

2. If the government had banned cigarettes, _____

   _____

   _____

3. If a risk is a result of a natural cause, _____

   _____

   _____

4. If people had no perception of risk, _____

   _____

5. If patterns of risk perception are the same for all cultures, _____

   _____

   _____

6. If the U.S. government had known about the terrorist attacks on the
   Twin Towers, _____

   _____

7. If we are threatened, _____

   _____

8. If our lives were safer, _____

   _____

9. If we were logical about risk, _____

   _____

   _____

10. If scientists had eliminated mad cow disease, _____

    _____

    _____

The following sentences are based on Reading 2. Choose the best word from the box to complete each sentence, and write a definition of the word on the line underneath the sentence. The first one has been done for you.

abated (v.)	evidence* (n.)	phenomenon* (n.)	respond* (v.)
annual* (adj.)	evolution* (n.)	predict* (v.)	trigger* (v.)
circumstances* (n.)	factors* (n.)	rampant (adj.)	ultimately* (adv.)
confers* (v.)	genders* (n.)	react* (v.)	unique* (adj.)

* Appears on the Academic Word List

1 By the summer of 2001, though the virus continued to show up and make a few people sick, the fear had _____*abated*_____.

DEFINITION: *weakened or ended*

2 What is frightening to you might not be to your friend. Neither of you is right or wrong. You just each have a _____ perspective.

DEFINITION: _____

3 The belief is supported by the fact that patterns of risk perception cross cultures, age groups, _____ and other demographic groupings.

DEFINITION: _____

4 Many people took broad-spectrum antibiotics even though they had no _____ that they had been exposed to anthrax—but they didn't get an _____ flu shot.

DEFINITION: _____

DEFINITION: _____

5 These are deeply ingrained patterns, probably ancient behaviours imprinted on us over millions of years of _____.

DEFINITION: _____

6 There are several _____ that influence our perceptions
   of risk.

   DEFINITION: _____

7 In the fall of 2001, awareness of terrorism was so high that fear was
   _____, while fear of street crime and global climate
   change and other risks was low, ... because awareness was down.

   DEFINITION: _____

8 Those variations make sense, too, because different people have different
   lives, different jobs, different family _____, different sets
   of experiences, different sets of values and so on.

   DEFINITION: _____

9 Fearing a risk more if it involves children, for example, means parents will
   _____ differently from, say, teenagers.

   DEFINITION: _____

10 The psychological study of this _____, known as "risk
   perception," explains why our fears often don't match the facts.

   DEFINITION: _____

11 Most people are less afraid of risks if the risk also _____
   some benefits they want.

   DEFINITION: _____

12 Essentially, any given risk has a set of identifiable characteristics that help
   _____ what emotional responses that risk will
   _____.

   DEFINITION: _____
   DEFINITION: _____

13 But do these judgments make sense? Are they rational? They are not based
   simply on the facts. But this is how humans _____ to
   risk ... with our hearts as well as our heads.

   DEFINITION: _____

14 The facts about risk are only part of the matter. _____,
   we react to risk with more emotion than reason.

   DEFINITION: _____

What Makes Us Afraid?

Read the following questions and use the read smart techniques you learned in Chapter 3 (page 56) to find the answers. When you have finished, discuss your answers with a small group of students. Make sure your answers are complete. Discuss any differences you might have.

❶ Why is it important to have accurate information about risks?

_____

_____

❷ Use your knowledge of conditional sentences to list the main factors that increase our perception of risk (making us more afraid) and that decrease our perception of risk (making us less afraid) in the following table. For some points in the reading, you may be able to write an entry in both sides of the table. Use your own words to paraphrase.

FACTORS THAT INCREASE OUR PERCEPTION OF RISK	FACTORS THAT DECREASE OUR PERCEPTION OF RISK
If risks are new, they are more frightening than old risks.	

❸ Which of these risk perception factors apply to the case of Susan Napolitano in Reading 1?

_____

_____

_____

_____

❹ How does risk perception play a role in evolution?

_____

_____

❺ What explains individual differences in risk perception?

_____

_____

Public Risk Perception

"People are disturbed, not by things, but by the view they take of them."
—Epictetus, Greek philosopher, 55–135 CE

The facts about risk are only part of the matter. Ultimately, we react to risk with more emotion than reason. We take the information about a risk, combine it with the general information we have about the world and then filter those facts through the psychological prism of risk perception. What often results are judgments about risk far more informed by fear than by facts.

The terrorist attacks on the World Trade Center in New York and on the Pentagon and the subsequent anthrax attacks in the fall of 2001 are an example. Many of us were afraid, and rightly so. But some people responded by driving to a distant destination rather than flying, even though the facts clearly showed that flying remained the far safer mode of transportation, even after September 11. Some people bought guns, raising their risks from firearms accidents far more than reducing their risk of being attacked by a terrorist. Many people took broad-spectrum antibiotics even though they had no evidence that they had been exposed to anthrax—but they didn't get an annual flu shot.

Do these judgments make sense? Are they rational? They are not based simply on the facts. But this is how humans respond to risk … with our hearts as well as our heads. The psychological study of this phenomenon, known as "risk perception," explains why our fears often don't match the facts.

Humans tend to fear similar things, for similar reasons. Scientists studying human behaviour have discovered psychological patterns in the subconscious ways we "decide" what to be afraid of and how afraid we should be. Essentially, any given risk has a set of identifiable characteristics that help predict what emotional responses that risk will trigger. Here are a few examples of what are sometimes called "risk perception factors."

- Most people are more afraid of risks that are new than those they've lived with for a while. In the summer of 1999, New Yorkers were extremely afraid of West Nile virus, a mosquito-borne infection that killed several people and that had never been seen in the United States. By the summer of 2001, though the virus continued to show up and make a few people sick, the fear had abated. The risk was still there, but New Yorkers had lived with it for a while. Their familiarity with it helped them see it differently.

- Most people are less afraid of risks that are natural than those that are human-made. Many people are more afraid of radiation from nuclear waste, or cellphones, than they are of radiation from the sun, a far greater risk.

- Most people are less afraid of a risk they choose to take than of a risk imposed on them. Smokers are less afraid of smoking than they are of asbestos and other indoor air pollution in their workplace, which is something over which they have little choice.

50 • Most people are less afraid of risks if the risk also confers some benefits they want. People risk injury or death in an earthquake by living in San Francisco or Los Angeles because they like those areas, or they can find work there.

- Most people are more afraid of risks that can kill them in particularly awful ways, like being eaten by a shark, than they are of the risk of dying in less awful ways, 55 like heart disease—the leading killer in America.

- Most people are less afraid of a risk they feel they have some control over, like driving, and more afraid of a risk they don't control, like flying, or sitting in the passenger seat while somebody else drives.

- Most people are less afraid of risks that come from places, people, corporations 60 or governments they trust, and more afraid if the risk comes from a source they don't trust. Imagine being offered two glasses of clear liquid. You have to drink one. One comes from Oprah Winfrey. The other comes from a chemical company. Most people would choose Oprah's even though they have no facts at all about what's in either glass.

65 • We are more afraid of risks that we are more aware of and less afraid of risks that we are less aware of. In the fall of 2001, awareness of terrorism was so high that fear was rampant, while fear of street crime and global climate change and other risks was low, not because those risks were gone, but because awareness was down.

70 • We are much more afraid of risks when uncertainty is high and less afraid when we know more, which explains why we meet many new technologies with high initial concern.

- Adults are much more afraid of risks to their 75 children than risks to themselves. Most people are more afraid of asbestos in their kids' school than asbestos in their own workplace.

- You will generally be more afraid of a risk that could directly affect you than a risk that 80 threatens others. U.S. citizens were less afraid of terrorism before September 11, 2001, because up till then the Americans who had been the targets of terrorist attacks were almost always overseas. But suddenly on September 11, 85 the risk became personal. When that happens, fear goes up, even though the statistical reality of the risk may still be very low.

People who learn about these risk perception patterns often remark on how much sense they seem

90 to make. It's little wonder. These are deeply ingrained patterns, probably ancient behaviours imprinted in us over millions of years of evolution. Long before we had our modern thinking brain, long before humans or primates even developed, only organisms that could recognize and successfully respond to danger survived and evolved. In Darwinian terms, these affective, "irrational" ways of protecting ourselves

95 are adaptive. They help us preserve the species. Evolution selects for this type of behaviour. The belief is supported by the fact that these patterns of risk perception cross cultures, age groups, genders and other demographic groupings. There are some variations among individuals. Those variations make sense too because different people have different lives, different jobs, different family circumstances,

100 different sets of experiences, different sets of values and so on. Fearing a risk more if it involves children, for example, means parents will react differently from, say, teenagers. What is frightening to you might not be to your friend. Neither of you is right or wrong. You just each have a unique perspective on the same statistics and facts. But risk perception research shows that underneath our individual differences,

105 we share certain patterns of risk response.

Ropeik, D., & Gray, G. (2002). *Risk: A practical guide for deciding what's really safe and what's really dangerous in the world around you* (pp. 15-18). Boston, MA: Houghton Mifflin Company.

Academic
Survival Skill

Avoiding Plagiarism by Summarizing

Plagiarism is copying another person's words or ideas. In Chapter 5, you found out how to avoid plagiarism by quoting and providing a reference for the quotation. In Chapter 6, you learned how to avoid plagiarism by paraphrasing and providing a reference. Another useful way to avoid plagiarism is by summarizing and providing a reference.

Learning how to summarize is an essential skill for students because professors may ask for formal, written summaries in order to evaluate students' writing skills. In addition, summarizing information is an efficient way to study.

Like a paraphrase, a summary translates another person's ideas into your own words. However, unlike a paraphrase, a summary is approximately one third of the original writing's length. To write a summary, therefore, you must summarize the main points of the writing and eliminate all the details and examples.

To write a summary, try this approach:
• Before beginning your summary, read the original source carefully. Underline only the main points of the writing.
• Begin your summary by referring to the author, title and source of the article.
• Paraphrase the underlined sections of the original source.
• Eliminate the details, examples and repetitious points from your summary.
• Write a reference to acknowledge the ideas contained in your summary.

A. With one or two classmates, on a separate sheet of paper practise summarizing the following text. Follow the steps for summarizing. Refer to the Models Chapter (page 191) to see an example of a summary and to learn more about how to write one. Include the reference for this text in your summary.

B. When you have finished, write your summary on the board. Look for successful summarizing techniques in each summary. As a class, write a single summary that combines the best features of each of the summaries.

Living from one moment to the next forces us to make judgments and decisions when we don't have all the facts, or enough time to get all the facts, or the intelligence necessary to understand all the facts. This concept is called *bounded rationality*, the process by which we make judgments and decisions without perfect knowledge. The subconscious tricks we use to make choices and judgments under conditions of bounded rationality play a huge role in how we respond to risk. Our risk response is, after all, a matter of judgment, not some cold, hard, fully factual logical analysis. That sort of perfect rationality is a myth, an idea. In real life, rationality is bounded, limited. It can take us only so far.

Ropeik, D. (2010). *How risky is it, really? Why our fears don't always match the facts* (p. 23). New York, NY: McGraw Hill.

WARM-UP ASSIGNMENT
Write a Short Summary

Summarize the following text. Write your summary on a separate sheet of paper. Use the academic perspective (third-person, present tense). Pay careful attention to subject-verb and pronoun-antecedent agreement. Use correct verb forms in conditional sentences. Don't forget to include the reference for the text at the end of your summary.

There is a lot of argument over whether people who are too afraid of smaller risks or not afraid enough of bigger ones are being irrational. Susan Napolitano's fear of the negligible risk from the air in her daughter's school, for example, and her lack of concern about smoking and obesity, certainly seemed to fly in the face of reason. Her judgments were not good for her health. The people who blame too much emotion and lack of reasoning for people's irrational choices—businesspeople, political conservatives, regulators, scientists, engineers and many academics—often claim, with no small amount of condescension and frustration, that people like Susan who get risk "wrong" are [just not smart. Their] thinking is described as "flawed" or "fallible" …

> When you receive feedback from your teacher or your classmates on this Warm-Up Assignment, you will have some information that you can use to improve your writing on the Final Assignment.

On the other hand, some people argue that too much cold rationality in decision-making, often based on dollars and cents, inappropriately ignores our values and feelings. Environmentalists, consumer advocates, social activists and political liberals hold that [emotional] thinking is fine. They argue that while some of our judgments about risk may not conform to all the scientific facts, they are based on a combination of the facts and our perspectives, informed by our feelings and instincts and experiences and cultural values, and that those are all valid parts of deciding how best to protect ourselves in a complex, risky world. They argue that there is nothing at all irrational about that sort of thinking.

Ropeik, D. (2010). *How risky is it, really? Why our fears don't always match the facts* (pp. xix–xx). New York, NY: McGraw Hill.

A. The words listed in the first column of the following table are from Reading 3. Match each word to the best definition.

B. When you have finished, check your answers with the class.

KEY WORD	DEFINITION
1 altered* (v.)	___1___ changed
2 anecdotal (adj.)	_____ forced
3 confined* (v.)	_____ probably
4 distorted* (adj.)	_____ in spite of the fact just mentioned
5 epidemiological (adj.)	_____ information printed in a book, magazine, etc., so the public can read it
6 equivalent* (adj.)	_____ belief about what is right and what is wrong
7 established* (adj.)	_____ restricted or limited
8 furor (n.)	_____ changed in appearance so it is unclear
9 hierarchy* (n.)	_____ identical, the same
10 imposed* (adj.)	_____ based on a personal story
11 incidence* (n.)	_____ showing how diseases are transmitted
12 interventions* (n.)	_____ differ
13 licensing* (n.)	_____ done willingly without being forced
14 media* (n.)	_____ happening in many places at once
15 nevertheless* (adv.)	_____ approval to own or do something for a period of time
16 presumably* (adv.)	_____ existing for a long period of time
17 principle* (n.)	_____ frequency or rate, the number of times something happens
18 publication* (n.)	_____ involvements in a problem in order to make the situation better
19 vary* (v.)	_____ system of organization that places more important things at the top and less important things at the bottom
20 voluntary* (adj.)	_____ all the organizations that provide information to the public, such as radio, television, newspapers, Internet
21 widespread* (adj.)	_____ sudden expression of anger among a large group of people about something that has happened

*Appears on the Academic Word List

A. Read the following text, which has been divided into four sections based on content. Skim each section, and with a partner, write a heading that reflects the content of the section. When you have finished, discuss your headings with the class.

Vaccination

Section 1: _____

Resistance to immunization is based on the belief that it gives rise to adverse reactions. Of course no interventions are entirely safe. However, the incidence
5 of severe adverse reactions to vaccines is extremely rare. The smallpox vaccine was one of the more hazardous vaccines. It caused encephalomyelitis in about 1 in 10,000 vaccinated subjects; and in rare, immunodeficient children, it could result in progressive vaccinia, which was often fatal. However, because smallpox was so dreaded, this incidence of adverse reaction was generally regarded as
10 acceptable …

There has been a public furor about reports that autism and an unusual form of colitis may be associated with the MMR vaccine (the combined vaccine against measles, mumps and rubella). This is based on a report by Wakefield et al … which gave an anecdotal description of twelve children where the onset of symp-
15 toms was said to be associated with the vaccine. Subsequent epidemiological studies have failed to show any association. Of these three diseases, measles is by far the most dangerous. Measles interferes with immunity mechanisms and, particularly in undernourished populations, kills many children usually from a subsequent bacterial infection. It can also give rise to encephalomyelitis and to
20 deafness. Furthermore, in approximately 1 in 500,000 children (and in the order of 1 in 20,000 children who catch measles before the age of two), measles infection is followed after some years by an extremely distressing, lethal brain disease

known as *subacute sclerosing panencephalitis* (SSPE). It has been shown that the incidence of SSPE is reduced at least tenfold by vaccination against measles. For
25 measles …, therefore, the risk … of vaccination must be very low. Mumps is a much less severe disease but can be very unpleasant, particularly if acquired after early childhood, and it is therefore well worth immunizing against. Rubella in childhood is a harmless disease, and the main reason for immunizing the population against rubella is to prevent the infection of pregnant women, which leads
30 to severe abnormalities in the unborn child. Widespread rubella vaccination has been very successful in reducing this fetal rubella syndrome. Since none of these diseases are close to being eradicated, the reduction in uptake of the vaccines that has followed the publication of the Wakefield work has led to an epidemic of measles and an increase of serious complications and deaths.

35 It is interesting that the problems with the MMR vaccination are confined largely to the United Kingdom. On the other hand, in France there has been a scare about the association of hepatitis B vaccination with multiple sclerosis. Hepatitis B is a serious liver disease, which if caught early in life predisposes to liver cancer and where later infection can trigger cirrhosis. The development of a vaccine against
40 hepatitis B using recombinant surface antigen has been a great success story, and the vaccine is widely used. The association with multiple sclerosis is again entirely anecdotal, and epidemiological studies show no association. Nevertheless, the French government has altered its hepatitis B vaccination recommendations on the basis of this scare.

45 *Section 2:* _____

Why is it that the public reacts so strongly to these vaccine scares although the real benefit is so large? One reason is clearly that the vaccine-damaged child is a real child whose picture can appear in the media and with whom people can identify. On the other hand, the "vaccine-saved" children, who do not get sick as a result of
50 being vaccinated, are only statistics and their impact is much less.

A second more plausible argument is used by some more sophisticated parents. If all other children are immunized, then the disease will become so uncommon that their children will not need immunization. Although there is a truth in this argument, it fails as soon as it is used by more than a tiny minority.

55 Thirdly, there are pressures from anti-vaccination groups who object to vaccination as a matter of principle … To some extent these anti-vaccination groups may regard all preventative medicine as "playing God" and believe that one should be fatalistic about infectious disease. For others it may simply be a strong mistrust of the pharmaceutical industry and of medicine in general. The anti-vaccination movement
60 certainly comes from the same sort of background as the groups opposed to rational medicine and to the genetic modification of food and to the fluoridation of water.

Another argument often used against vaccination is the "precautionary principle." This principle, though very widely quoted, has no agreed definition. It is often used in the sense that nothing should be done until it can be shown with a very high degree of
65 certainty that no possible harm can result from it. It is therefore often used as a reason for preferring inaction to action whenever there is any uncertainty. However in some

situations, for example, climate change, the precautionary principle is used as an argument for taking positive prevention actions even when there is still uncertainty as to whether it may be necessary. However, action and inaction in public health are morally 70 equivalent. It is no better to cause harm by doing nothing than by doing something …

Section 3: _____

Others have discussed why risk tolerance varies so much between different risky activities. It seems clear that risk tolerance is much higher for voluntary than imposed risk. People accept much 75 higher risks in car travel than they do in rail travel … It is also clear that risk tolerance is much higher when there is individual benefit. For example, mobile phones are tolerated much 80 more readily than genetically modified food where the benefit to the individual is not so apparent.

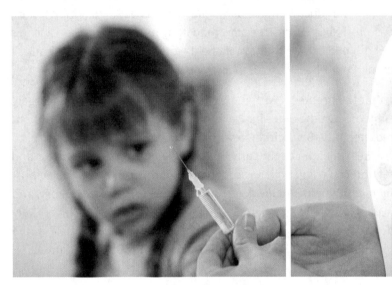

There is also clearly a hierarchy of activities, which vary in their acceptability 85 of risk. Taking part in sport, such as sailing, horse riding, mountain climbing or football, entails much higher risks than would be tolerated in driving cars or riding bicycles. There is, in its turn, much higher risk tolerated in therapeutic pro- 90 cedures such as surgical operations than is tolerated in drugs or food; and vaccination appears to attract the highest risk intolerance of all. Finally, there is the fear of unknown secondary effects, for example starting an epidemic.

Section 4: _____

The risk reduction costs of these different activities must also be very different. The 95 amount it costs to save one extra life on roads and railways is roughly known … On the railways it is said to be of the order of two million pounds [CAN$3.16 million] per life saved and on roads probably rather less than this. The costs in late drug development for saving one extra life are probably higher than this, and for vaccines the cost is not known but is presumably higher again. For example, making an already 100 safe vaccine even safer will involve re-licensing the new product. The trials needed for this purpose will be enormously expensive …

Section 5: _____

Vaccination provides a powerful example where the public perception appears to be very distorted from the established realities. It is, therefore, a good example for 105 studying how such disconnections come about.

Reference

Wakefield, A.J., Murch, S.H., Anthony, A. et al. (1998). Ilial-lymphoid-nodular hyperplasia, non-specific colitis, and pervasive developmental disorder in children. *Lancet, 351* (9103), 637–41.

Lachmann, P.J. (2002). Vaccination. In A. Weale (Ed.), *Risk, democratic citizenship and public policy* (pp. 94–98). Oxford, UK: Oxford University Press.

B. Still working with your partner, answer the following questions about the text. When you have finished, discuss your answers with the class.

1 Does the author of this text believe the risks of vaccination are acceptable? How do you know?

_____

_____

_____

2 Why does the author think the risks of the smallpox vaccine were acceptable?

_____

_____

_____

3 How does the author suggest that the Wakefield et al study that showed the MMR vaccine caused autism (a mental disorder) was not reliable?

_____

_____

_____

4 Why does the public respond with such strength to questions of vaccine safety?

_____

_____

_____

5 What are some of the reasons for people's willingness to accept some risks and not others?

_____

_____

_____

_____

6 What point about the costs of risk reduction is the author trying to make in the second last paragraph?

_____

_____

_____

_____

7 Should governments assume the cost of eliminating all public risk? Why or why not?

_____

_____

_____

_____

Identifying Cause and Effect

In Reading 3, there are many words or expressions that connect a *cause* to an *effect*.

A. Read the examples in the table, and then, using the words or expressions, complete the sentences that follow. The first one has been done for you.

WORD OR EXPRESSION	SENTENCE IN READING 3
cause	The smallpox vaccine was one of the more hazardous vaccines. It **caused** encephalomyelitis in about 1 in 10,000 vaccinated subjects.
give rise to	Resistance to immunization is based on the belief that it **gives rise to** adverse reactions.
lead to	Rubella in childhood is a harmless disease, and the main reason for immunizing the population against rubella is to prevent the infection of pregnant women, which **leads to** severe abnormalities in the unborn child.
result in/from/of	On the other hand, the "vaccine-saved" children, who do not get sick **as a result of** being vaccinated, are only statistics and their impact is much less.
trigger	Hepatitis B is a serious liver disease, which if caught early in life predisposes to liver cancer and where later infection can **trigger** cirrhosis.

① After the MMR scare in the United Kingdom, the decline in immunization

_____*triggered*_____ an increase in measles, mumps and rubella

infections.

② Climate change_____

_____

_____

③ Some people are worried that radiation from cellphones will_____

_____

_____

④ Complications from measles_____

_____

_____

⑤ If a pregnant woman contracts rubella, it_____

_____

_____

6 Some people say that the hepatitis B vaccine _____

_____

_____

7 Governments state that paying more money to eradicate all risks will

_____

_____

B. When you want to express a connection that is weaker than cause and effect, use the expression that the writer used frequently in Reading 3: "be associated with." This is a good expression to use when you want to suggest there is doubt about the connection between the cause and the effect. Read the examples, and then use the expression to complete the sentences that follow.

EXPRESSION	SENTENCE IN READING 3
may be associated with	There has been a public furor about reports that autism and an unusual form of colitis **may be associated with** the MMR vaccine.
was said to be associated with	This is based on a report by Wakefield et al ... which gave an anecdotal description of twelve children where the onset of symptoms **was said to be associated with** the vaccine.

1 After some child swimmers developed polio, there was concern that

swimming _____

_____

_____

2 Once several vaccinated people developed the flu, the flu vaccine

_____

_____

_____

FINAL ASSIGNMENT
Write a Summary

Summarize Section 2 of Reading 3 (page 151 and 152). Use the summarizing techniques you learned in this chapter and vocabulary related to risk perception. Write conditional sentences and use words or expressions of cause and effect as required.

Refer to the Models Chapter (page 191) to see an example of a summary and to learn more about how to write one.

CHAPTER 8

The Slow Food Movement

How often do you make your own meals and eat them with friends and family? How often do you shop at a market for fresh, locally grown food?

Participants in the Slow Food movement try to do these things daily. They also believe that buying locally grown food is the best way to enjoy tasty food, ensure sustainable production and support local farmers. The Slow Food movement is more than simply a reaction to the prevalence of fast food and the speed of modern living. Advocates encourage a personal, agricultural and economic balance that may save our planet.

In this chapter,
you will

- learn vocabulary related to the Slow Food movement;

- select vocabulary to express your opinion;
- learn how to express critical thinking;

- learn tips to help you make sense of very long sentences;
- write persuasive essays.

GEARING UP

A. Are you a gastronome? If you are not sure what a gastronome is, read the following characteristics of gastronomes, as defined by Carlo Petrini, the founder of the Slow Food movement. Check the ones that apply to you.

CHARACTERISTICS OF GASTRONOMES	YES	NO	SOMETIMES
Insist on and take pleasure in eating good-quality food	☐	☐	☐
Appreciate food diversity and seek out new culinary experiences	☐	☐	☐
Avoid fast food (e.g., McDonald's) and object to it on principle	☐	☐	☐
Search for like-minded friends with whom they can share *good, clean* and *fair* food	☐	☐	☐
Have an interest in learning about and understanding the complexity of the systems that bring food to our tables	☐	☐	☐
Believe that food should be produced in a sustainable way that does not damage the Earth	☐	☐	☐
Believe farmers should be paid a reasonable wage for the food they produce, to bring a new dignity to food production	☐	☐	☐
Believe that many of the world's problems are a result of our methods of food production	☐	☐	☐

B. Discuss your answers with the class. Which characteristics are the most important for you and your classmates?

Read the words in context in the left-hand column, and write the parts of speech (*n. = noun, v. = verb, adj. = adjective, adv. = adverb*) and definitions in the right-hand column. The first one has been done for you.

WORDS IN CONTEXT	DEFINITION
1 Slow Food is the new **happy meal**.	happy meal: (___n.___) McDonald's meal for children
2 Canadians in their twenties **revel in** preparing homemade meals the "**old-fashioned**" way.	revel in: (_____)
	old-fashioned: (_____)
3 The twenty-three-year-old revels in the **labour*** associated with producing quality food.	labour: (_____)
4 Just the thought of travelling to a farmer's market and labouring over a stove to prepare an evening **feast** may be enough to **tempt** some people to dial their nearest fast-food restaurant.	feast: (_____)
	tempt: (_____)
5 Mass-market food is generally priced to **conform** to a student-friendly budget and is easily **accessible*** for those who don't have the ability to travel farther afield to shop.	conform: (_____)
	accessible: (_____)
6 Students take part in a garden program that ties into many **aspects*** of school life.	aspects: (_____)
7 We have a population of youth who are questioning the influence of **corporate*** power in all aspects of life.	corporate: (_____)
8 The youth **chapter*** will be the latest addition to a movement that's been steadily growing since 1989, when Slow Food International was **founded**.*	chapter: (_____)
	founded: (_____)
9 She **acknowledges*** there are **inherent*** challenges for youth who want to get away from mass-market food.	acknowledges: (_____)
	inherent: (_____)

▶

WORDS IN CONTEXT	DEFINITION
⑩ Canada's Slow Food movement is an **initiative*** meant to promote sustainable food production and encourage stronger communities.	initiative: (_____)
⑪ The famous chef joined with educational **institutions*** in the province to expose students of all ages to Slow Food values.	institutions: (_____)
⑫ The Slow Food movement says its primary goal is to **promote*** environmental and community awareness through the pleasures of good food.	promote: (_____)
⑬ Youth can also stretch their dollars further by **teaming up with** friends to share more expensive food **resources**.*	teaming up with: (_____)
	resources: (_____)
⑭ Stephanie Kolk—along with a few like-minded youthful **foodies**—is in the process of launching a Slow Food "**convivium**" geared **specifically*** toward young people in southern Alberta.	foodies: (_____)
	convivium: (_____)
	specifically: (_____)
⑮ The convivium's **inaugural** event … will be a simple "eat–in," where guests bring ingredients and collaborate to produce a meal.	inaugural: (_____)
⑯ He **laments** the loss of home-cooking skills, which are lost as busy parents increasingly reach for simple mealtime solutions.	laments: (_____)
⑰ As **culinary** skills disappear, cultural roots and community supports go with them, he said.	culinary: (_____)

*Appears on the Academic Word List

READING ❶ Slow Food in Canada

Read the following questions and then read the text to answer the questions. When you have finished, compare your answers with those of a partner. Then, discuss them with the class.

❶ What type of text are you reading, and what helps you identify it?

_____

_____

_____

▶

② What does Stephanie Kolk like to do, and why does she think it is important?

_____

_____

_____

③ What are Slow Food advocates (like Kolk) planning for young people in Calgary? What will participants do there?

_____

_____

_____

④ Why does De Campo think the Slow Food movement is opposed to corporate power?

_____

_____

_____

⑤ How are people participating in the Slow Food movement in Nova Scotia, Canada?

_____

_____

_____

⑥ Kolk identifies some inherent challenges for young people who want to get away from mass-market food. What are these challenges?

_____

_____

_____

⑦ What are some possible solutions to these inherent challenges?

_____

_____

_____

⑧ Is there a Slow Food chapter in your area? If so, when and where does it meet?

_____

_____

_____

"Slow Food" the New Happy Meal by M. McQuigge

Canadians in their twenties revel in preparing homemade meals the "old fashioned way."

Just the thought of travelling to a farmer's market and labouring over a stove to pre-
5 pare an evening feast may be enough to tempt some people to dial their nearest fast-food restaurant, but a dinner prepared the old-fashioned way is Stephanie Kolk's idea of a happy meal.

The twenty-three-year-old revels in the labour associated with producing quality food, particularly when she can be involved at every step of the process.

10 For Kolk, collecting home-grown tomatoes from a local greenhouse, dicing them for a caprese salad or simmering and seasoning them to turn
15 them into the perfect pomodoro sauce are all part of the joy of cooking. It's a pleasure she fears too many members of her generation are missing
20 out on as they stand in line to buy a sandwich or reheat the contents of a package bought at a supermarket.

Kolk hopes to pull her generation back into the kitchen by introducing them to
25 Canada's "Slow Food" movement, an initiative meant to promote sustainable food production and encourage stronger communities.

"We need to educate ourselves so we can educate the next generation," Kolk said in a telephone interview from Calgary.

"Food has gotten so broken down. Almost nobody lives on farms anymore. It's gotten
30 out of fashion to grow your own food. Without some training and education, the next generation could have some serious troubles with the food system."

Kolk—along with a few like-minded youthful foodies—is in the process of launching a Slow Food "convivium" geared specifically toward young people in southern Alberta.

Participants will take part in events that further the understanding of how food is
35 grown and prepared. Farm tours and market excursions will be on the agenda, but Kolk said the primary focus will be on building a community. The convivium's inaugural event—scheduled for later this month—will be a simple "eat-in," where guests bring ingredients and collaborate to produce a meal.

The youth chapter will be the latest addition to a movement that's been steadily
40 growing since 1989, when Slow Food International was founded.

The Italy-based organization, which now has chapters in 150 countries, says its primary goal is to promote environmental and community awareness through the pleasures of good food.

Paul De Campo, who headed up Toronto's Slow Food chapter for nearly five years,
45 said youth engagement has been a rising focus of Canadian participants. He laments the loss of home-cooking skills, which are lost as busy parents increasingly reach for simple mealtime solutions.

As culinary skills disappear, cultural roots and community supports go with them, he said.

De Campo is optimistic that the Slow Food movement may catch on; particularly in
50 the wake of "Occupy" protests that raised awareness of the impact big business has on everyday life.

"We have a population of youth who are questioning the influence of corporate power in all aspects of life, and Slow Food is certainly about addressing and pushing back on the corporate control of our food system," De Campo said.

55 Michael Howell, a chef based in Wolfville, NS, recognized the importance of mobilizing youth to take charge of the food supply long before the tents were pitched in Zuccotti Park. Fearing the influence of slick marketing campaigns and mis-leading packaging, he joined forces with educational institu-
60 tions in the province to expose students of all ages to Slow Food values.

The first campus convivium was held at Acadia University and is scheduled to expand to Dalhousie in the coming months, he said.

65 Students at Dr. Arthur Hines Elementary School in Summer-ville, NS, meanwhile take part in a garden program that ties into many aspects of school life, he said. Students grow food in the garden, allowing them to acquire key scientific and nutritional knowledge. That food is then harvested and served
70 in the school's cafeteria.

Howell believes schools are ideal targets for food intervention, since they represent pre-established communities of young people with both physical and intellectual hungers to satisfy.

"It seems not just reasonable but really important for Slow
75 Food to come together in an area where food production is part of everybody's life," he said.

Kolk acknowledges there are inherent challenges for youth who want to get away from mass-market food, which is gen-erally priced to conform to a student-friendly budget and
80 easily accessible for those who don't have the ability to travel farther afield to shop.

She believes, however, that solutions exist for those who take the time to educate themselves. Canning and pickling fresh produce purchased in the summer can save time and money
85 through the winter months, she said, adding youth can also stretch their dollars further by teaming up with friends to share more expensive food resources. Such efforts naturally promote social engage-ment that appeals to so many of Canada's young people, she said, adding some will be surprised by how inclusive a movement it can be.

90 "Slow Food isn't an activist group," she said. "We're not standing around with signs yelling at people. It's about connecting lives and food. It's about creating a community."

"It's great fun and it's awesome, and there are more benefits to it than just organic vegetables."

McQuigge, M. (2012, January 11). "Slow food" the new happy meal. *Waterloo Region Record* (p. E2).

FOCUS ON WRITING

Selecting Vocabulary to Express Opinions

As you know, writers write about facts, but they might also express their opinions about facts. When writers use expressions such as "in my opinion" or "I believe that," it is easy to identify their opinions. However, these are first-person expressions that are not always appropriate to use in academic writing. Nevertheless, writers manage to express their opinions in their academic writing. How do they do it?

Read the following sentence from Reading 2, in which the writer expresses his disgust with modern methods of food production. How do you, the reader, know the writer's opinion?

> "Chemical fertilizers and pesticides, intensive feeding, antibiotic digestive enhancers, growth hormones, rigorous breeding, genetic modification—every scientific trick known to man has been deployed to cut costs, boost yields and make livestock and crops grow more quickly."

The writer has used the word "trick" to refer to methods used in commercial farming. The word "trick" as it is used here has a negative connotation—a negative meaning beyond the actual definition of the word. By using this word, the author is expressing his opinion that modern food production is an unnatural or unfair game used to increase efficiency. If the writer had used the word "method," the reader would not have the same understanding of the writer's opinion.

Here is another sentence from Reading 2. Again, the writer expresses his dissatisfaction with modern methods of food production. What words does the author use to express his opinion?

> "Two centuries ago, the average pig took five years to reach 286 kilograms; today, it hits 484 kilograms after just six months and is slaughtered before it loses its baby teeth."

The words "hits" and "slaughtered" convey to the reader the writer's opinion. The clause "before it loses its baby teeth" also suggests that the animal is being killed at too young an age. Consider how different your understanding would be if the writer wrote the sentence this way:

> Two centuries ago, the average pig took five years to reach 286 kilograms; today, it weighs 484 kilograms after just six months and is *butchered while the meat is still tender*.

You might expect to find this sentence in a text about the benefits of modern methods of food production. You would think that the writer approves of these methods.

You can see that careful selection of vocabulary can be used to express opinion without the use of the first person. Now, read one more sentence from Reading 2 and underline the words that express the writer's opinion.

> "The small landowner gives way to the factory farm, which churns out food that is fast, cheap, abundant and standardized."

Working with a partner, read the following sentences about modern methods of food production. The sentences are neutral; they do not express an opinion. Keeping the facts the same, replace some of the words with synonyms that have negative connotations, to express unhappiness with modern methods of food production. When you have finished, compare your answers with the class.

1 Today, North American salmon are genetically modified to grow four to six times faster than they would in the wild.

_____

_____

_____

2 With new strains of rice, farmers can grow two or more harvests of grain within a single year.

_____

_____

_____

3 There are varieties of peaches that can be picked when they are hard and shipped over long distances.

_____

_____

_____

READING ❷   In Praise of Slowness

As you might guess, this writer advocates strongly for the Slow Food movement; he compares farmers to artists by writing about artisanal (related to artists) production and artisanal food. His opposition to speed in all things is reflected in his title "Turning the Tables on Speed." This expression ("to turn the tables on something") means to reverse the situation to gain an advantage.

Read the text and answer the questions that follow.

Turning the Tables on Speed

Today, most meals are little more than refuelling pit stops. Instead of sitting down with family or friends, we often eat solo, on the move or while doing something else—working, driving, reading the newspaper, surfing the Net. Nearly half of Britons now eat their
5 evening meal in front of the TV, and the average British family spends more time together in the car than they do around the table. When families do eat together, it is often at fast-food joints like McDonald's, where the average meal lasts eleven minutes …

The acceleration at the table is mirrored on the farm. Chemical fertilizers and pesticides, intensive feeding, antibiotic digestive enhancers, growth hormones, rigorous
10 breeding, genetic modification—every scientific trick known to man has been deployed to cut costs, boost yields and make livestock and crops grow more quickly. Two centuries ago, the average pig took five years to reach 286 kilograms; today, it hits 484 kilograms after just six months and is slaughtered before it loses its baby teeth. North American salmon are genetically modified to grow four to six times faster than

15 the average. The small landowner gives way to the factory farm, which churns out
food that is fast, cheap, abundant and standardized.

As our ancestors moved into the cities and lost touch with the land, they fell in love
with the idea of fast food for a fast age. The more processed, the more convenient,
the better … Many of us have swallowed the idea that when it comes to food, faster
20 is better. We are in a hurry, and we want meals to match. But many people are waking
up to the drawbacks of the "gobble, gulp and go" philosophy. On the farm, in the
kitchen and at the table, they are slowing down. Leading the change is an international
movement with a name that says it all: Slow Food …

It all started in 1986, when McDonald's opened a branch beside the famous Spanish
25 Steps in Rome. To many locals, this was one restaurant too far … To roll back the
fast-food tsunami sweeping across the planet, Carlo Petrini, a charismatic culinary
writer, launched Slow Food. As the name suggests, the movement stands for everything that McDonald's does not: fresh, local, seasonal produce; recipes handed down
through the generations; sustainable farming; artisanal production; leisurely dining
30 with family and friends. Slow Food also idealizes "eco-gastronomy"—the notion that
eating well can, and should, go hand in hand with protecting the environment …

Petrini thinks this is a good starting point for tackling our obsession with speed in all
aspects of life. The group states: "A firm defence of quiet material pleasure is the only
way to oppose the universal folly of Fast Life … Our defence should begin at the table
35 with Slow Food."

With its very modern message—eat well and still save the planet—Slow Food has
attracted seventy-eight thousand members in more than fifty countries. In 2001, the
New York Times named it one of the "eighty ideas that shook the world …" Aptly enough,
Slow Food takes the snail as its symbol, but that does not mean the members are lazy
40 or sluggish …

All over the world, Slow Food activists organize dinners, workshops, school visits and
other events to promote the benefits of taking our time over what we eat. Education is
key. In 2004, Slow Food opened its own University of Gastronomic Sciences at Pollenzo,

near Bra, Italy, where students study not only the science of food
45 but also its history and sensual character. The movement has already persuaded the Italian state to build "food studies" into the school curriculum. In 2003, Petrini himself helped the German government lay the groundwork for a nationwide "taste education" program.

On the economic side, Slow Food seeks out artisanal foods that are
50 on the way to extinction and helps them find a place in the global market. It puts small producers in touch with one another, shows them how to … promote their products to chefs, shops and gourmets around the world. In Italy, over 130 dying delicacies have been saved, including lentils from Abruzzi, Ligurian potatoes, the
55 black celery of Trevi, the Vesuvian apricot and purple asparagus from Albenga … Similar rescue operations are underway in other countries. Slow Food is working to save the Firiki apple and traditional olive oil-soaked ladotiri cheese in Greece. In France, it has advocated for the Pardigone plum and a delicate goat's cheese
60 called Brousse du Ruve.

As you might expect, Slow Food is strongest in Europe, which has a rich tradition of indigenous cuisine and where fast-food culture is less strongly established. But the movement is also growing across the Atlantic. Its American membership is eight thousand
65 and rising. In the United States, Slow Food helped persuade *Time* magazine to run a feature on the Sun Crest peach of northern California, a fruit that tastes sublime but travels badly. After the article appeared, the small producer was overwhelmed with buyers wanting to sample his crop. Slow Food is also leading a successful campaign to bring back the tasty rare-breed turkeys—Naragansett, Jersey
70 Buff, Standard Bronze, Bourbon Red—that were the centrepiece of every American family's Thanksgiving supper until bland factory-farmed birds took over …

As part of its ecological beliefs, Slow Food opposes the genetic modification of foodstuffs and promotes organic farming. Nobody has conclusively proven that organic food is more nutritious or better tasting than non-organic, but it is clear that the methods used
75 by many conventional farmers take a toll on the environment, polluting the water table, killing off other plants and exhausting the soil. According to the Smithsonian Migratory Bird Center in the United States, pesticides, directly or indirectly, kill at least sixty-seven million American birds every year. By contrast, a well-run organic farm can use crop rotation to enrich the soil and manage pests—and still be very productive.

80 Slow Food fights for biodiversity. In the food industry, efficiency leads to homogenization: manufacturers can process inputs—be they turkeys, tomatoes or turnips—more quickly if they are all the same. So the farmers are required to concentrate on single strains or breeds. Over the last century, for instance, the number of artichoke varieties grown in Italy has tumbled from two hundred to about a dozen. Besides narrowing
85 our choice of flavours, the loss of animal variety upsets delicate ecosystems … In addition, when all you have is one breed of turkey, a single virus can wipe out the whole species.

Honoré, C. (2004). *In praise of slowness: How a worldwide movement is challenging the cult of speed* (pp. 54–63). San Francisco, CA: HarperSanFrancisco.

1 To increase efficiency, what "scientific tricks" must farmers use, and what benefits do they achieve?

_____

_____

_____

2 How did the Slow Food movement start?

_____

_____

_____

3 Globally, what do Slow Food activists do?

_____

_____

_____

4 Why does the Slow Food movement support organic farming and oppose genetic modification?

_____

_____

_____

5 Why does the Slow Food movement support biodiversity?

_____

_____

_____

WARM-UP ASSIGNMENT
Write a Short Persuasive Essay

In order to prepare for your Final Assignment, write a short persuasive essay that either agrees with or disagrees with the following statement.

> The Slow Food movement will improve the condition of the environment.

Remember that a persuasive essay should try to convince your readers to accept your viewpoint. Select vocabulary that expresses your opinion without using the first-person perspective. Refer to the Models Chapter (page 185) to see an example of a persuasive essay and to learn more about how to write one.

When you receive feedback from your teacher or your classmates on this Warm-Up Assignment, you will have some information that you can use to improve your writing on the Final Assignment.

The following sentences are based on Reading 3. Choose the best word from the box to complete each sentence, and write a definition of the word on the line underneath the sentence. The first one has been done for you.

*abandoned** (v.)	crucial* factor (n.)	ensure* (v.)	procuring (v.)
contradiction* (n.)	despite* (prep.)	incompatible* (adj.)	radical* (adj.)
contributed* (v.)	element* (n.)	intensification* (n.)	ranges* (v.)
convinced* (adj.)	emerging* (adj.)	modes* (n.)	sphere* (n.)
cultivated (adj.)	empirical* evidence (n.)	previously* (adv.)	valid* (adj.)

* Appears on the Academic Word List

1. In some places, agriculture has been _____*abandoned*_____ because it was not profitable.

   DEFINITION: *left behind, stopped*

2. Food production is rising, the amount of _____ land is increasing, and 22 percent of the world population (almost half of the total workforce) is engaged in agriculture.

   DEFINITION: _____

3. During the past twenty years, we have used more than twice as many chemical fertilizers as we had ever _____ produced!

   DEFINITION: _____

4. Agriculture today consists of an _____ of a few crops, to the detriment of a magnificent genetic diversity created through millennia of experimentation.

   DEFINITION: _____

5. _____ the evidence of the adverse consequences of large-scale industrial agriculture, it has become the dominant model.

   DEFINITION: _____

6. Agricultural monocultures (farms that produce only one strain of plant or one breed of animal) are _____ from the commercial point of view but have eliminated agricultural diversity.

   DEFINITION: _____

7. Modern agriculture has created a simplification of nature in order to minimize uncertainty and _____ an efficient production of commercial goods.

   DEFINITION: _____

▶

⑧ There has been a continual reduction in the number of animal breeds and vegetable varieties that have for centuries _____ to feeding and supporting entire regions.

DEFINITION: _____

⑨ Traditional practices have demonstrated that other _____ of production are possible.

DEFINITION: _____

⑩ Man is _____ that he can dominate nature and that it is entirely at his service.

DEFINITION: _____

⑪ Unsustainable methods of food production ... have since turned the _____ of food and agriculture into a neglected sector ...

DEFINITION: _____

⑫ People should still regard food as a central _____ in our lives.

DEFINITION: _____

⑬ The complex quality of food is a concept that _____ from the question of taste to that of variety, from respect for the environment, ecosystems and the rhythms of nature to respect for human dignity.

DEFINITION: _____

⑭ There is _____ that agro-industry is not fulfilling its promise of eradicating world hunger.

DEFINITION: _____

⑮ Agro-industry is a model of food production that is _____ with the needs of the planet.

DEFINITION: _____

⑯ Agriculture has become completely detached from the lives of billions of people, as if _____ food required no effort at all.

DEFINITION: _____

⑰ The formulas of chemical fertilizers ... have been the _____ in the escalation of modern industrial agriculture and its unnaturalness.

DEFINITION: _____

⑱ Slow Food demands a _____ change in mentality, more complexity of thought, more humility and a greater sense of responsibility toward nature.

DEFINITION: _____

▶

19 The words "agriculture" and "industry" can be combined to form the term *agro-industry*. But this must be a _____. Agriculture should not conform to the principles of industry.

DEFINITION: _____

20 The _____ problem is this: agro-industry has given us the illusion that it could solve the problem of feeding the human race when clearly it cannot.

DEFINITION: _____

READING ③ — A Slow Food Nation

This text was written by Carl Petrini, the founder of the Slow Food movement. It has been translated from Italian. Read the following questions and then read the text to answer the questions. When you have finished, compare your answers with those of a partner. Then, discuss them with the class.

1 Why does Petrini think that something has gone wrong with modern agriculture?

_____

_____

_____

2 Petrini writes that modern methods of agro-industry have made food production both executioner and victim. What does he mean?

_____

_____

_____

3 Why does Petrini argue that food must regain its central place in our lives?

_____

_____

_____

4 What does Petrini blame Western agriculture for?

_____

_____

_____

5 What are the dangers of creating an agricultural monoculture?

_____

_____

_____

6 Why is the term *agro-industry* a contradiction?

_____

_____

_____

7 What damage does the "final balance sheet" display?

_____

_____

_____

8 What should be the characteristics of a new agriculture?

_____

_____

_____

9 What does Petrini believe the situation demands now?

_____

_____

_____

Restoring Food to Its Central Place

Food production is rising, the amount of cultivated land is increasing, and 22 percent of the world population (almost half of the total workforce) is engaged in agriculture, but the food produced for twelve billion people is in fact not enough to feed the six 5 billion who actually live in the world. Moreover, this effort of production has not achieved its aims. It has subjected the Earth to such stress that the land either turns to desert or dies because of the excessive use of chemical products. Water resources are running out. Biodiversity is rapidly diminishing, especially agro-biodiversity, with a continual reduction in the number of animal breeds and vegetable varieties that 10 have for centuries contributed to the sustenance of entire regions in a perfectly sustainable partnership between man and nature.

Something must have gone wrong, because if we consider the problem of satisfying the primal need for food and analyze it over the long term, the hunger for production has done more harm than good.

15 The contradiction in agro-industrial terms is clearly emerging: agro-industry has given us the illusion that it could solve the problem of feeding the human race. I would go even further: over the last fifty years, it has turned food production into both executioner and victim. Executioner, because the unsustainable methods of agro-industry

have led to the disappearance of many sustainable production methods that were
20 once part of the identity of the communities that practised them and were one of the
highest pleasures for the gastronome in search of valuable knowledge and flavours.
Victim, because the same unsustainable methods—originally necessary in order to
feed a larger number of people—have since turned the sphere of food and agriculture
into a neglected sector, completely detached from the lives of billions of people, as
25 if procuring food … required no effort at all. Politicians show little interest in it, except
when pressured to do so by the most powerful international corporations of agro-
industry, while the average consumer either does not reflect on what he or she is
eating or has to make a titanic effort to obtain the information that will explain it.

Food and its production must regain the central place that they deserve among human
30 activities, and we must re-examine the criteria that guide our actions. The crucial
point now is no longer, as it has been for all too long, the quality of food that is produced, but its complex quality, a concept that ranges from the question of taste to
that of variety, from respect for the environment, ecosystems and the rhythms of
nature to respect for human dignity. The aim is to make a significant improvement
35 to everybody's quality of life without having to submit, as we have done until now,
to a model of development that is incompatible with the needs of the planet.

Agro-Industry?

It should be stated at the beginning that if food is to regain its central place, we will
have to concern ourselves with agriculture. It is impossible to discuss food without
40 discussing agriculture. Every gastronome should be aware of this because the present
situation in the world is the result of the history of Western agriculture (and the damage
it has done to nature), an agriculture that has lost sight of some of the aims that are
most important to anyone who cares about the quality of food …

The formulas of chemical fertilizers were first developed in the 1840s, and they have
45 been the crucial factor in the escalation of modern industrial agriculture and its
unnaturalness.[1] The trend toward chemistry did not just carry on the tradition of
introducing elements alien to existing ecosystems but introduced inorganic elements
that have been overused. During the past twenty years, we have used more than twice
as many chemical fertilizers as we had ever previously produced! Can the Earth sustain
50 such a change in its balance?

As Debal Deb stated in a 2004 publication, modern agricultural and forestry sciences
have created a simplification and homogenization of nature in order to minimize
uncertainty and ensure an efficient production of commercial goods; agriculture today
consists of an intensification of a few crops, to the detriment of a magnificent genetic
55 diversity created through millennia of experimentation. The monocultures of those
varieties that are valid from the commercial point of view have shaped modern agriculture, which rapidly eliminates life forms, impoverishes the soil and destroys the
systems that support life on Earth. The worst thing, Deb goes on to say, is that, despite
the empirical evidence of the adverse consequences of large-scale industrial agricul-
60 ture, this has become the model to follow for agricultural development in all the
countries that try to imitate the Western model of growth.[2]

---

1. Bevilacqua, P. (2002). *La mucca è savia* (p. 22). Rome, IT: Donzelli.

2. Deb, D. (2004). *Industrial vs. ecological agriculture* (p. 4). New Delhi, IN: Navdanya/Rfste.

The absurd idea (it is a contradiction in terms!) of industrial agriculture—agriculture carried out according to the principles of industry—is thus dominant. Under industrial agriculture, the fruits of nature are considered raw materials to be consumed and 65 processed on a mass scale. The subversion of the natural order has affected the entire food production system. The agro-industry of food production has become the model of development in a world in which technology reigns. And if it has done enormous damage in the Western world that invented it, the imposition of a single method of development … has created even worse problems elsewhere. It has done untold harm 70 to the environments and people of the countries that are poorest in material wealth (though certainly not in biodiversity), and to traditions and cultures that have existed for centuries in perfect harmony with their ecosystems …

The final balance sheet is beginning to show the effects of these changes: enormous damage caused to the ecosystem; an increase in food production that has not solved 75 the problems of hunger and malnutrition; and an incalculable loss from cultural and social points of view. From this latter viewpoint, ancient traditions and knowledge have been thrown away; the rural population has abandoned the countryside to fill up the cities (a phenomenon that is reaching catastrophic proportions in developing countries, creating megalopolises like New Delhi or Mexico City); and there has been 80 a loss of culinary knowledge that was once the basis of a correct—as well as enjoyable—use of agricultural resources. We are witnessing a form of cultural destruction that has affected the countryside of every part of the world, on a scale that has never before been seen in human history.

There is therefore an urgent need for 85 new kinds of farming, a truly *new agriculture*. Sustainable methods can take their starting point from the small (or large, depending on where in the world you are) amount of knowledge 90 that has not been eliminated by agro-industrial methods. This will not be a return to the past, but rather a new beginning that grows out of the past, with an awareness of the mistakes 95 that have been made in recent years. It will involve making productive again those areas where agriculture has been abandoned because it was not profitable according to industrial cri-100 teria; preserving, improving and spreading knowledge of the traditional practices that are demonstrating that other modes of production are possible; and giving new dignity and new 105 opportunities to the people who have been marginalized by the globalization of agriculture.

Only through a new sustainable agriculture that respects both old traditions and modern technologies (for the new technologies are not bad in themselves—it all 110 depends on how one uses them) can we begin to have hopes of a better future. And only through its global acceptance will gastronomes be able to move from their present state of protesters against the prevailing trends to that of fulfilled people who still regard food as a central element in our lives.

The Gastronome

115 There is a theory that man, since he is convinced that he can dominate nature and that it is entirely at his service, finds solutions through technology, but that with every technological answer he invents, he in fact creates new and more serious problems. I would say that this is true of the Earth today, and we seem to have reached the absolute limit.

120 This situation demands much more than a simple change, of course: it demands a radical change in mentality, more complexity of thought, more humility and a greater sense of responsibility toward nature.

Petrini, C. (2005). *Slow food nation: Why our food should be good, clean, and fair* (pp. 22–28). New York, NY: Rizzoli Ex Libris.

FOCUS ON READING

Reading Multi-Clause, Multi-Phrase Sentences

You may have noticed that Reading 3 was challenging to read because the writer used many long sentences. These sentences contain multiple clauses and phrases that can make the sentences difficult to understand. You can help yourself make sense of these long sentences by identifying the start and end points of the clauses and phrases in the sentence.

Each clause and phrase packages content to help you, the reader, understand.

Here is the first sentence of the reading. Underline each clause.

> "Food production is rising, the amount of cultivated land is increasing, and 22 percent of the world population (almost half of the total workforce) is engaged in agriculture, but the food produced for twelve billion people is in fact not enough to feed the six billion who actually live in the world."

As you can see, the sentence begins with three independent clauses that are linked by commas and the coordinate conjunction *and*.

The writer is using the commas to show the reader he is combining independent clauses as items in a series. The coordinate conjunction *but* (preceded by a comma) shows that the writer is starting another independent clause that presents contrasting information. And finally, the relative pronoun *who* introduces an adjective clause that describes the preceding noun *six billion (people)*.

It is the punctuation and conjunctions that help the reader understand the content and the construction of the sentence.

▶

If you find you need to reread long sentences several times to understand them, highlight the punctuation and conjunctions in the sentence to help you divide the content. Here is another long sentence from Reading 3. Underline the clauses and prepositional phrases to show how the content is packaged in this sentence.

> "Biodiversity is rapidly diminishing, especially agro-biodiversity, with a continual reduction in the number of animal breeds and vegetable varieties that have for centuries contributed to the sustenance of entire regions in a perfectly sustainable alliance between man and nature."

In this sentence, the independent clause is extended with a prepositional phrase ("with a continual …"), an adjective clause beginning with *that* (to describe the vegetable varieties) and another prepositional phrase ("in a perfectly …"). Recognizing the divisions between the clauses and phrases can help you understand the meaning of the sentence more easily.

Working with a partner, underline the clauses and phrases in the following sentences. Circle the conjunctions, relative pronouns and prepositions that signal the divisions between clauses and phrases. When you have finished, discuss the meaning of the sentences with the class.

1. Executioner, because the unsustainable methods of agro-industry have led to the disappearance of many sustainable production methods that were once part of the identity of the communities that practised them and were one of the highest pleasures for the gastronome in search of valuable knowledge and flavours.

2. Victim, because the same unsustainable methods—originally necessary in order to feed a larger number of people—have since turned the sphere of food and agriculture into a neglected sector, completely detached from the lives of billions of people, as if procuring food required no effort at all.

3. Politicians show little interest in it, except when pressured to do so by the most powerful international corporations of agro-industry, while the average consumer either does not reflect on what he or she is eating or has to make a titanic effort to obtain the information that will explain it.

4. As Debal Deb stated in a 2004 publication, modern agricultural and forestry sciences have created a simplification and homogenization of nature in order to minimize uncertainty and ensure an efficient production of commercial goods; agriculture today consists of an intensification of a few crops, to the detriment of a magnificent genetic diversity created through millennia of experimentation.

Academic
Survival Skill

Expressing Opposing Ideas

The texts in this chapter have presented a positive view of the Slow Food movement and its benefits. Suppose your instructor now asks you and your classmates to consider some possible negative consequences of the Slow Food movement. If, for example, everyone adopted slow food as a philosophy of life and of economic and environmental balance, what might some of the negative consequences be?

In response you might list the following concerns:

1. "Slow Food farming" means not using fertilizers or pesticides to grow food. This will reduce farmers' production, leading to lower incomes.

2. "Slow Food farming" means not shipping produce over long distances. This will conserve fuel, but it also means some foods will not be available in some countries. For example, it may be difficult to get fruit and vegetables in the winter in countries with cold climates.

3. "Slow Food farming" means diversifying animal and plant varieties rather than standardizing strains. This could lead to higher food prices.

4. "Slow Food cooking" means shopping for fresh food and spending time preparing a meal in the old-fashioned way. It is likely these activities will be done by women, who may already be busy with family and work.

Your instructor then asks you to write about these concerns. You may feel uncomfortable writing negatively about a movement that seems to have so many advantages. You may feel that your negative concerns are not significant or that you don't want to criticize such a popular movement. And you may feel that academic writing should just deal with the facts, and not with a writer's opinion. However, in many academic communities, it is appropriate and necessary to express divergent opinions about topics to show you are capable of independent thought. Your challenge is how to appropriately express views that oppose those of other writers.

Here are some "sentence frames" that will help you express opposing thoughts.

Use the active voice to oppose a specific writer.

Although/even though Petrini believes that ..., he has not considered ...

Petrini states that ...; however, he must also think about ...

Scholars/researchers continue to disagree about Petrini's statement that ...

Scholars/researchers dispute/take issue with Petrini's suggestion that ...

Critics of the Slow Food movement differ sharply with Petrini's conclusion that ...

Petrini is mistaken when he states that ...

Use the active voice to oppose an idea.

Women are divided on the issue of ...

There is disagreement/dispute about how ...

There is controversy about ...

This ... is a contentious issue in the Slow Food movement.

This ... is a divisive issue in the Slow Food movement.

Use the passive voice to avoid criticizing the writer(s) directly.

Not enough thought/consideration has been given to ...

More thought/consideration should be given to ...

Not enough attention has been given to ...

More attention should be given to ...

Despite ..., not enough importance has been attached to ...

Despite ..., more importance should be given to ...

A. Can you think of other ways to express opposition to a writer or an idea? If so, share them with the class.

B. Use the sentence frames to express opposition to the Slow Food movement. You can use the opposing ideas previously mentioned, or you may be able to think of other points of opposition. When you have finished, write your sentences on the board and discuss their effectiveness with the class.

❶ _____

_____

_____

_____

❷ _____

_____

_____

_____

❸ _____

_____

_____

_____

❹ _____

_____

_____

_____

FINAL ASSIGNMENT
Write an Extended Persuasive Essay

Write a persuasive essay of approximately three to four pages. Whichever position you take in your essay, express the opposing view as well, using the sentence frames above.

Agree or disagree with one of the following statements, and explain why.

❶ If more people adhere to the Slow Food movement, it will be beneficial to women.

❷ If more people adhere to the Slow Food movement, it will reduce the cost of food.

❸ If more people adhere to the Slow Food movement, it will be beneficial for the environment.

❹ If more people adhere to the Slow Food movement, it will ensure farmers are paid more for the food they produce.

Refer to the Models Chapter (page 185) to see an example of a persuasive essay and to learn more about how to write one.

MODELS CHAPTER

This chapter provides models of the writing assignments that you may be required to write as you progress through this textbook. All of the assignments are about water, allowing you to see how the same information can be arranged to meet the demands of different writing assignments.

Before each model assignment,

you will find

- instructions that highlight the key characteristics of the writing assignment;

- the outline that the writer used to prepare for the writing assignment.

MODEL 1 **How to Write Short Answers**

In the first sentence,

- repeat the important words from the question;

- respond to the first word in the question (for example, *what, when, why, how, explain, define*).

In the rest of the short answer,

- provide correct and detailed information to answer the question;

- organize the information (for example, first to last, simple to complex).

Question 1: What is the water cycle?

WRITER'S PLAN
• sky to Earth to sky (vapour to liquid to vapour) • rain and snow falls • falls on ground, rivers and oceans • evaporates from land and returns to atmosphere

Answer

The **water cycle** is the process of water movement from the sky to the Earth and back to the sky again. Water is a vapour in the atmosphere, but changes to liquid rain or solid snow as it falls to Earth. Once on land, the water flows into the earth, rivers and oceans. The water will then evaporate and become a vapour again as it returns to the atmosphere.

Question 2: What are the differences between a watershed and an aquifer?

WRITER'S PLAN	
WATERSHED	AQUIFER
• all land from which water drains into a common body of water • is natural—not based on political borders • example	• water in the ground • water travels downwards until it hits rock • aquifer is the layer of water above the layer of rock • can be large or small • example

Answer

A **watershed** is all the land from which water drains into a common body of water while an **aquifer** is an underground layer of water found just above a layer of rock.

A **watershed** is a natural dividing line that does not reflect political borders. As a result, countries may share watersheds. Canada and the United States share a number of watersheds, such as the Pacific Watershed west of the Rocky Mountains that drains into the Pacific Ocean, and the Great Lakes-St. Lawrence watershed that drains into the Atlantic Ocean.

An **aquifer**, or layer of water stored underground, is created as water from rain or melting snow sinks into the ground. Aquifers are important because people drill wells down to the aquifer to find water. Canada and the United States also share a number of large aquifers.

Question 3: How can we conserve water around our homes?

WRITER'S PLAN
TWO WAYS TO CONSERVE WATER • use less water—repair, collect rain, be water-efficient • avoid contamination—use non-toxic cleaners, reduce pesticide and salt use

Answer

People can conserve water around their homes in two ways. First, they can use less water. By repairing leaky taps and toilets, collecting and using rainwater, reducing water use for the lawn and using water-efficient shower heads and taps, people can save a significant amount of water. Second, people must avoid contaminating their water supply with toxic cleaners, fertilizers, pesticides and salt.

MODEL 2   How to Design a Survey

A survey is designed to collect information from people (respondents/participants). To create a survey, you should

• decide what information you want to gather (limit yourself to finding out one or two pieces of information);

- select two different groups of respondents you want to find out information about (for example, men and women, older and younger, Chinese and Canadian);
- write a *hypothesis* (a sentence that explains what you expect to discover);
- ask five or six questions that will give you the information you want, including yes/no questions, multiple-choice questions or Likert scale questions (to which participants can answer a) always, b) often, c) sometimes, d) rarely, e) never);
- write the questions so that you can easily record the respondents' answers;
- conduct the survey (ask the survey questions);
- ask the same number of respondents from each of the groups;
- summarize the information in a table;
- consider whether your hypothesis was correct and try to explain the outcome(s) based on the information you have gathered.

Example Survey

Hypothesis: *Older people use more water than younger people.*

1. How old are you?

   ☐ thirteen to thirty   ☐ thirty-one and over

2. How many showers or baths do you take per day?

   ☐ one or less   ☐ two   ☐ more than two

3. On average, how many times do you flush the toilet per day?

   ☐ one to three times   ☐ four or five times   ☐ six times or more

4. How many times per week do you use the clothes washer?

   ☐ once or less   ☐ twice   ☐ more than twice

5. How many times per week do you use the dishwasher?

   ☐ once or less   ☐ twice   ☐ more than twice

6. Do you water your lawn?

   ☐ yes   ☐ no

Summary of Survey Results

QUESTIONS	TOTAL NUMBER AGED THIRTEEN TO THIRTY (TEN)			TOTAL NUMBER AGED THIRTY-ONE AND OVER (TEN)		
1 How old are you?	**% TOTAL** 50%			**% TOTAL** 50%		
2 How many showers or baths do you take per day?	**<1 or 1** 7	**2** 3	**2>** 0	**<1 or 1** 10	**2** 0	**2>** 0
3 On average, how many times do you flush the toilet per day?	**1–3** 0	**4–5** 8	**6>** 2	**1–3** 0	**4–5** 4	**6>** 6
4 How many times per week do you use the clothes washer?	**<1 or 1** 5	**2** 5	**2>** 0	**<1 or 1** 0	**2** 0	**2>** 10
5 How many times per week do you use the dishwasher?	**<1 or 1** 2	**2** 7	**2>** 1	**<1 or 1** 0	**2** 0	**2>** 10
6 Do you water your lawn?	**YES** 0		**NO** 10	**YES** 4		**NO** 6

How to Write a Report

A report is designed to explain data or information. The following guidelines will help you write an effective report.

- Divide the report into sections. Many reports are divided into *introduction, methods, results* and *discussion* sections. However, your sections will depend on the information that you need to explain.

- Select logical section headings.

- In your introduction section, explain why the information was collected.

- In your methods section, explain how the information was collected.

- In your results section, explain what you discovered. You may include tables or charts in this section.

- In your discussion section, highlight the value of the report's results, mention any limitations of the report and provide your ideas for further research.

Example Report on the Model Survey

WRITER'S PLAN	
INTRODUCTION	• general information about fresh water • importance of conservation • importance of public education campaigns to encourage water conservation • segment of the population that would be best to target with these campaigns • hypothesis
METHODS	• explain survey design • explain participant selection (by age)

RESULTS	• hypothesis correct
	• summarize major results:
	  - younger people have showers more frequently
	  - older people use toilets, dishwashers, clothes washers and lawn sprinklers more frequently
	  - overall, older people use more water than younger people

DISCUSSION	• limitations: is water use related to age or size of household • more research needs to be done to target water reduction campaigns effectively

Introduction

Water conservation is becoming an important issue as world population increases. Although the world is covered with water, 97 percent of that water is salt water, and much of the remaining 3 percent is held in glaciers in the North and South Poles. Only a small percentage of the Earth's water is available to support human life. Water conservation is essential if people want to preserve their quality of life. The expression, "Think globally, act locally," encourages individuals to reduce their water consumption.

Scientists and governments are trying to educate people to reduce their water consumption and protect the quality of existing water. In order to do this, individuals should use less water by repairing leaky taps, collecting and using rainwater, buying water-efficient bathroom fixtures, eliminating grass-watering and reducing the use of toxic cleaners, fertilizers, pesticides and salts. Although most people are aware they should be conserving water, many people do not actually make an effort to reduce their water consumption where it counts most: in the home. The public needs to be educated about how to reduce and protect water.

To develop effective public education campaigns, it is important to know who uses the most water. Do older people use more water than younger people? If this is true, then the government can target older people with its water use reduction campaigns. If younger people use more water, then the government can target younger people in these campaigns. This survey was based on the hypothesis that older people (aged thirty-one and over) used more water than younger people (aged thirteen to thirty).

Method

The survey was designed to cover all the areas where water is often wasted in the home: showers (baths), toilets, clothes washers, dishwashers and lawns. There was one question for each of these areas. Here is a list of the questions.

1. How old are you?
   (This question divided the respondents into "younger" or "older" age groups.)

2. How many showers or baths do you take per day?

3. On average, how many times do you flush the toilet per day?

4. How many times per week do you use the clothes washer?

5. How many times per week do you use the dishwasher?

6. Do you water your lawn?

Showers (which use up to 100 litres per five-minute shower),[1] toilets (which use up to 19 litres per flush), clothes washers (which use up to 225 litres per wash), dishwashers (which use up to 40 litres per wash) and lawn sprinklers (which use up to 36 litres per minute) consume a large amount of water per day. These questions were designed to find out if the individuals were using less or more water.

Twenty people completed the survey. These people were selected, based on their age, so that half the survey population was between thirteen and thirty, and half was older than thirty. Children younger than thirteen were not surveyed because these individuals probably do not have the responsibility for cleaning their homes and clothes, and therefore, probably use less water than adults, who have greater responsibility in these areas.

Results

The results prove the hypothesis correct. Older people (aged thirty-one and over) use more water than younger people (aged thirteen to thirty). For only one question (Question 2), the results show that older people use less water than younger people; more senior people have fewer showers per day, consuming less water in this area only. The answers to the third question demonstrate that older individuals consume

---

1. All estimates taken from Project Blue, Roots and Shoots, Canada Water Campaign (2008). Water in Canada. Retrieved from: http://www.janegoodall.ca/project-blue/WaterinCanada.html

slightly more water than younger individuals by flushing the toilet more times per day. One hundred percent of both older and younger people said they flushed the toilet more than four times per day, yet 60 percent of older people flushed more than six times per day compared to only 20 percent of younger people. This suggests that more senior individuals are flushing slightly more often than younger individuals.

Responses to Questions 4 and 5 clearly show that older people use significantly more water per day than younger people. In response to the questions, "How many times per week do you use the clothes washer, and the dishwasher?" 100 percent of more senior people said they use these appliances more than twice a week. For these same questions, 100 percent of younger people said they used the clothes washer two times or less per week, and 90 percent said they used the dishwasher two times or less per week. These differences result in significantly reduced water consumption for younger people.

Similarly, when asked if they water their lawns, 100 percent of younger individuals responded "no" while only 60 percent of older individuals answered "no." As a result, younger people were again using less water than older people.

Discussion

The results support the hypothesis that older people use more water than younger people. Older participants used the toilet, clothes washer, dishwasher and sprinkler more frequently than younger respondents. Older individuals only used less water in the shower, as they had fewer showers than younger people.

It is possible that age is not the reason why more senior people use more water than more junior people. All the older respondents had children, and therefore larger households than the younger respondents. It is likely that having children results in more clothes and dishes to wash, and possibly more toilets to flush during the day. Of the younger people in the survey, only one of them had children. It is suggested that any follow-up survey should divide the respondents according to whether they have children or not.

More research should also be done to determine whether water reduction campaigns should be aimed at younger or older people, or if some other segment of the population should be the focus of encouragement to reduce water use.

MODEL 4 How to Write a Process Essay

Process essays are written to explain *how* something is done. Therefore, often a process essay explains the steps in a process. The following guidelines will help you write an effective process essay.

• Like all essays, a process essay must have three general sections: an introduction, a body and a conclusion. Unlike a report, you may not use these section titles as headings in the essay.

• The introduction announces the topic of the essay. Although there are many good ways to start an essay, the introduction usually begins with a general statement about why the topic is important.

• The introduction finishes with a *thesis statement*. A thesis statement is a sentence that includes the topic of the essay and the opinion that the essay will present. It may or may not include the main steps of the process that you are writing about.

- The body of the essay will contain a number of paragraphs. For a short process essay, usually each paragraph describes one step in the process.
- Each body paragraph should start with a topic sentence that clearly indicates the topic of the paragraph. If your thesis listed the main steps of the process, you can repeat the key words (or a form of the key words) from the thesis.
- Each body paragraph should finish with a sentence that makes the point of the paragraph clear.
- The conclusion summarizes the main steps in the process. It often finishes with a sentence that restates (but not repeats) the thesis.

Example Process Essay

How is dirty water cleaned for drinking?

WRITER'S PLAN	
INTRODUCTION	NOT MUCH WATER AVAILABLE FOR USE • dirty water must be cleaned and reused • this is the water treatment process • three steps: sedimentation, filtration and disinfection
BODY	• sedimentation removes tiny particles from the water: alum is added; water thickens; particles stick together and sink to the bottom • filtration: water is passed through a sand filter to remove any remaining waste • disinfection: chlorine is added to remove bacteria; fluoride is added
CONCLUSION	• three steps in the water treatment process provide clean drinking water

Cleaning our Water

Although the world is covered with water, 97 percent of that water is salt water, and much of the remaining 3 percent is held in glaciers in the North and South Poles. Only a small percentage of the Earth's water is available to support human life. This means it is important to use less water and avoid polluting water. It also means that people must clean dirty water if they want to have enough. The process of cleaning dirty water so that it is safe to drink is called *the water treatment process*. Dirty water is often treated by sedimentation, filtration and disinfection before it is clean.

Sedimentation of dirty water is the first step in the water treatment process. To start, a chemical called *alum* is mixed into the water to make small particles stick to each other. With gentle mixing, more and more small particles stick together. As a result, the heavy particles that are produced sink to the bottom of the tank, leaving the water cleaner, but not clean enough to drink.

After sedimentation, the water is filtered to remove the remaining particles. The water is passed through layers of stones, called *gravel*, and sand. These layers form a filter that further cleans the water. Once the water is through the filter, it is free of particles, but it is still not clean enough to drink.

To complete the water treatment process, disinfection destroys any bacteria or viruses that are present in the water. Chlorine, a chemical used to kill bacteria, is added to the water. Chlorine not only kills bacteria during the treatment process, but it also maintains the quality of the water as it is carried through the water distribution system.

Another chemical, fluoride, may be added to the water to help reduce tooth decay. The overall treatment results in water that is clean and ready to drink.

If dirty water is not treated properly, people and animals may become sick from the dirt and bacteria in the water. The water treatment process is constantly monitored to make sure this does not happen. An effective water treatment process that includes sedimentation, filtration and disinfection is essential if people want enough safe water to drink.

MODEL 5 How to Write a Persuasive Essay

Persuasive essays are written to persuade, or convince, people that a particular opinion about a topic is correct. The following guidelines will help you write an effective short persuasive essay.

- Like all essays, a persuasive essay must have three general sections: an introduction, a body and a conclusion. Unlike a report, you may not use these section titles as headings in the essay.

- The introduction announces the topic of the essay. Although there are many good ways to start an essay, the introduction usually begins with a general statement about why the topic is important.

- The introduction finishes with a *thesis statement*. A thesis statement is a sentence that includes the topic of the essay and the opinion that the essay will present. It may or may not include the main reasons why the opinion of the essay is correct.

- The body of the essay will contain a number of paragraphs. For a short persuasive essay, usually each paragraph explains one reason why the essay opinion is correct.

- Each body paragraph should start with a topic sentence that clearly indicates the topic of the paragraph. You can do this by repeating key words (or synonyms of the key words) from the thesis.

- Each body paragraph should finish with a sentence that makes the point of the paragraph clear.

- The conclusion summarizes the main reasons why the essay opinion is correct. It often finishes with a sentence that restates (but not repeats) the thesis.

Example Persuasive Essay

Water is becoming contaminated with a new form of pollution. Medicines (drugs or pharmaceuticals) used by humans and animals are entering the water system. Governments should make every effort to eliminate water pollution from pharmaceuticals. Agree or disagree and explain why.

WRITER'S PLAN	
INTRODUCTION	GENERAL INFORMATION • where: ground water, surface water and drinking water • what: types of medicines (pharmaceuticals) • source: humans and animals GOVERNMENTS SHOULD NOT ELIMINATE THIS FORM OF POLLUTION BECAUSE • pollution levels are low • money could be spent better elsewhere

▶

WRITER'S PLAN	
BODY	POLLUTION LEVELS VERY LOW • parts per billion, and parts per trillion • so much less than prescribed doses • only sensitive equipment allows us to find this kind of pollution VERY EXPENSIVE TO REMOVE MEDICINE POLLUTION FROM THE WATER • levels very low: hard to find, test and monitor • money could be spent better in researching the long-term effects of this pollution

CONCLUSION	• water pollution from pharmaceuticals is worrying
	• deserves further study, *but* remember
	  - pollution levels are low
	  - money could be spent better elsewhere

Water Pollution from Pharmaceuticals Requires More Study

It is well-recognized that water is essential for life, and consequently, water should be protected from pollution. In order to protect the water supply, water treatment processes are designed to eliminate many forms of harmful pollution. Recently, scientists have begun to find a new type of pollution in ground, surface and drinking water. They have discovered that human and animal medicines, such as antibiotics, are polluting the water. People expect governments to eliminate pollution from medicines or pharmaceuticals in their water. However, at the moment, governments should not attempt to remove medicines from the water supply because the levels of this kind of pollution are very low, and the removal of the pollution would cost money that could be spent on research.

The levels of pharmaceutical pollution in the water supply are extremely low. It is true that research in Europe and the United States has found some form of pharmaceutical pollution in almost all ground, surface and drinking water. However, measurements at levels this low have only become possible because of sensitive measurement equipment that was not available to scientists in the past. Scientists measure the amounts of pharmaceutical pollutants in parts per billion, and in some cases parts per trillion. These amounts of pollution from medicine are so low that they are unlikely to cause a crisis in health care in the short term.

In order to remove these low levels of pharmaceutical pollution from water, governments would have to spend a lot of money. The current water treatment processes remove many harmful particles and bacteria from the water, but they are not as effective at removing low levels of pharmaceutical pollution. Only advanced water treatment technologies would remove medicines from the water supply, and even then, some pharmaceuticals might not be eliminated. At this point, the money needed to remove all medicines from water would be better spent on research related to the long-term effects of pharmaceutical pollution on humans and animals.

Although the thought of medicines in the water supply is worrying, it would not be useful for governments to spend large amounts of money to change current water treatment processes to try to eliminate all pharmaceutical pollution. This kind of pollution is so minimal that it is difficult to measure. Furthermore, low levels of medicines are not likely to cause health problems in the short term. Instead of spending large amounts of money to modify water treatment processes, governments should spend money on research to identify the long-term effects of exposure to low levels of pharmaceuticals.

How to Write a Compare and Contrast Essay

Compare and contrast essays are written to show the similarities and differences between two items. When you compare items, you show the similarities; when you contrast items, you show the differences. The following guidelines will help you write effective compare and contrast essays.

- Decide what points of comparison or contrast you wish to explain to your reader.

- Decide which pattern of organization fits your information best. There are two standard ways to organize a compare and contrast essay: block style organization and point-by-point style organization. Generally, block style organization is best for less technical information while point-by-point style organization is best for more technical information. Both styles of organization are demonstrated here.

- Like other kinds of essays, a compare and contrast essay has three general sections: an introduction, a body and a conclusion. Unlike a report, you may not use these section titles as headings in the essay.

- The introduction announces the topic of the essay. Although there are many good ways to start an essay, the introduction usually begins with a general statement about why the topic is important.

- The introduction finishes with a *thesis statement*. A thesis statement is a sentence that includes the topic of the essay and the opinion that the essay will present. It may or may not include the main points of comparison or contrast.

- The body of the essay will contain a number of paragraphs. For a short compare and contrast essay, usually each paragraph explains one point of comparison or contrast.

- Each body paragraph should start with a topic sentence that clearly indicates the topic of the paragraph. You can do this by repeating key words (or synonyms of the key words) from the thesis.

- Each body paragraph should finish with a sentence that makes the point of the paragraph clear.

- The conclusion summarizes the points of comparison and/or contrast. It often finishes with a sentence that restates (but not repeats) the thesis.

Example Compare and Contrast Essay

Compare and contrast two different technologies that could be used to solve water shortages.

Block Style Essay

WRITER'S PLAN FOR A BLOCK STYLE COMPARE AND CONTRAST ESSAY	
• compare and contrast desalination with atmospheric water vapour processing - both are ways of producing pure drinking water - some differences in source, waste products and final product	
DESALINATION	ATMOSPHERIC WATER VAPOUR PROCESSING
• explain the process; give an example - source: ocean water - waste products: salty brine - final product: salty (transport inland)	• explain the process; give an example - source: water vapour in the air - waste products: none - final product: very pure
• desalination and water vapour processing are useful because - sources are accessible - few waste products - final product = drinking water	

Desalination and Atmospheric Water Vapour Processing

Desalination, or the process of removing salt from ocean water, and atmospheric water vapour processing, the process of turning water vapour into water, are both ways of producing drinking water for human consumption. Although desalination and atmospheric water vapour processing are distinct because they extract water from unique sources and produce different waste and final products, both are useful to increase the amount of water available for human use.

Producing drinking water from salty ocean water is the process of desalination. This process is used in the Middle East, where Saudi Arabia operates the largest desalination plant in the world. The source of water for desalination plants is ocean water. As ocean water is 97 percent of the world's water, there is a large supply of water that could be processed with desalination technology. The process does result in some unwanted waste products. Desalination plants produce salty brine, as well as some chemical wastes that must be properly disposed of. If the waste products are simply returned to the environment, they will pollute rivers and groundwater, but they can be properly managed so the environment is not damaged. Finally, the desalination process works by removing the salt from ocean water; however, it is impossible to remove all the salt. Therefore, the final product of desalination is drinking water with a salty taste.

Atmospheric water vapour processing pulls water vapour from the air, cools it and condenses it into drinking water. After an earthquake hit Taiwan in 1999, water vapour processors produced enough water to supply the military soldiers who were helping the relief efforts. The main source of water for this kind of treatment is humid air, which is free in large quantities. As for waste products, it is true that in order to cool the water vapour, a refrigerant is used. However refrigerants, also found in refrigerators and dehumidifiers, can be used for long periods of time before they become waste. The final product of atmospheric water vapour processing is appealing, too. It is one of the cleanest forms of water. Pollutants in the air that adhere to rain drops do not stick to water vapour; consequently, the final product of this process is very pure.

Both desalination and water vapour processing technology are useful methods for producing clean drinking water in countries where there is a lack of natural water supply. The sources of water for these processes are easily available, their waste products can be properly managed so they don't harm the environment, and the end products are clean drinking water for human consumption.

Jacobs, D. (2002, December 28). Water, water everywhere. *Ottawa Citizen*, p. A3.

Point-By-Point Style Essay

WRITER'S PLAN FOR A POINT-BY-POINT STYLE COMPARE AND CONTRAST ESSAY
• compare and contrast desalination with atmospheric water vapour processing - both ways of producing pure drinking water - some differences in source, waste products and final product

SOURCE OF WATER	• desalination: ocean water • water vapour processing: air

WASTE PRODUCTS	• desalination: salty brine • water vapour processing: none
FINAL PRODUCT	• desalination: tastes salty • water vapour processing: pure

• water vapour processing and desalination are useful because
  - sources are accessible
  - few waste products
  - final products = drinking water

Desalination and Atmospheric Water Vapour Processing

Desalination, or the process of removing salt from ocean water, and atmospheric water vapour processing, the process of turning water vapour into water, are both ways of producing drinking water for human consumption. Although desalination and atmospheric water vapour processing are distinct because they extract water from unique sources and produce different waste and final products, both are useful to increase the amount of water available for human use.

Each of these water creation technologies has a unique source of water. Producing drinking water from salty ocean water is the process of desalination. This process is used in the Middle East, where Saudi Arabia operates the largest desalination plant in the world. The main source of water for desalination plants is ocean water. As ocean water is 97 percent of the world's water, there is a large supply of water that could be processed with desalination technology. Alternatively, atmospheric water vapour processing pulls water vapour from the air, cools it and condenses it into drinking water. After an earthquake hit Taiwan in 1999, water vapour processors produced enough water to supply the military soldiers who were helping the relief efforts. The main source of water for this kind of treatment is humid air, which is free in large quantities. Each process is based on an abundant natural resource.

Every technology must be evaluated to determine if it produces waste products that will be dangerous to the environment. Desalination technology does result in some unwanted waste products: salty brine, as well as some chemicals. If the waste products are simply returned to the environment, they will pollute rivers and groundwater, but they can be properly managed so the environment is not damaged. Similarly, water vapour processing uses a refrigerant to cool the water vapour. However refrigerants, also found in refrigerators and dehumidifiers, can be used for long periods of time before they become waste. Both processes produce waste products that need to be disposed of properly.

The taste of the final product is also a significant consideration when evaluating water technologies. The desalination process works by removing the salt from ocean water; nevertheless, it is almost impossible to remove all the salt. Therefore, the final product of desalination is drinking water that tastes salty. In contrast, the final product of water vapour processing is one of the cleanest forms of water. Pollutants in the air that adhere to rain drops do not stick to water vapour; consequently, the final product of this process is very pure. However, both processes produce drinking water for human consumption.

Desalination and water vapour processing technology are useful methods for producing clean drinking water in countries where there is a lack of natural water supply. The sources of water for these processes are easily available, their waste products can be properly managed so they don't harm the environment, and the end products are clean drinking water for human consumption.

Jacobs, D. (2002, December 28). Water, water everywhere. *Ottawa Citizen*, p. A3.

MODEL 7   How to Write a Paraphrase

The goal of a paraphrase is to restate the ideas of another author without copying the author's words. Paraphrasing is an effective way to avoid plagiarism. Use the following guidelines to write a paraphrase.

- All paraphrases start with a reference to the original author. Common ways to start paraphrases are the following:

  In her 2012 article, (author's name) states that ...

  In his book of 2012, (author's name) suggests that ...

  According to (author's name) in her article of 2012, ...

  (Author's name) website maintains that ...

- A paraphrase is approximately the same length as the original writing.

- To restate the main ideas of an author without repeating the same words, you may use writing techniques such as finding synonyms for key words, changing the structure of the sentence, changing word forms and changing the voice from active to passive (or passive to active). See pages 120–122 for examples of these writing techniques.

- You may need to use more than one of these writing techniques to complete a successful paraphrase.

Example Paraphrase

Paraphrase the following text:

We tend to think of water in terms of a particular purpose: is the quality of the water good enough for the use we want to make of it? Water fit for one use may be unfit for another. We may, for instance, trust the quality of lake water enough to swim in it, but not enough to drink it. Along the same lines, drinking water can be used for irrigation, but water used for irrigation may not meet drinking water standards. It is the quality of the water which determines its uses.

Environment Canada (2010). Introduction to water quality. Retrieved from: http://www.ec.gc.ca/eau-water/default.asp?lang=En&n=2C3144F5-1

Example paraphrase:

> When we consider the uses to which water can be put, we must first determine its purity, states Environment Canada on its website (2010). A single source of water may not be suitable for all uses. For example, we may be sufficiently confident in a lake's water quality to swim; however, we would likely think twice before drinking it. Similarly, water pure enough to drink can be used for crops although not vice versa. Water use is dependent on its purity.

MODEL 8   How to Write a Summary

The goal of a summary is to restate the ideas of another author without copying the author's words. Summarizing, like paraphrasing, is an effective way to avoid plagiarism. Follow these guidelines to write a summary.

- All summaries, like paraphrases, start with a reference to the original author. Common ways to start summaries are the following:

  In her 2012 article, (author's name) states that …

  In his book of 2012, (author's name) suggests that …

  According to (author's name) in her article of 2012, …

  (Author's name) website maintains that …

- A summary, unlike a paraphrase, is approximately one quarter to one third the length of the original writing.

- To summarize an original text, you should:

  - read the original text carefully;

  - underline the main points of the original text, leaving out supporting details, repetitions and examples;

  - paraphrase the underlined sentences.

- To paraphrase the underlined sentences, you may use writing techniques such as finding synonyms for key words, changing the structure of the sentence, changing word forms and changing the voice from active to passive (or passive to active). See pages 120–122 for examples of these writing techniques.

- You may need to use more than one of these writing techniques to complete a successful summary.

Example Summary

Summarize the following text:

Each of us depends on water for our health, prosperity and enjoyment. We drink it, clean with it, swim in it, generate electricity with it and use it to grow food and put out fires. Since everything we do relies on a sustainable supply of water, it is essential that we protect this vital resource. As a country bordered by three oceans, the environmental well-being of fish, water mammals and other aquatic life is even more dependent on clean water than we are.

It's not surprising, in a country as rich in lakes and rivers as Canada, that so many Canadians take fresh water for granted. Canada is one of the highest water users per capita in the world. In 2006, Canadians used an average of 335 litres per day where residents of many European countries currently use less than 200 litres per day.

While Canada has 7 percent of the world's renewable fresh water, this water is not always available where needed. Canada's water challenge is that 85 percent of the Canadian population lives along the southern border but 60 percent of the country's fresh water flows to the north.

Environment Canada (2009). Water, water ... everywhere? Retrieved from: http://www.ec.gc.ca/envirozine/default.asp?lang=En&n=5D3C05E2-1

Example summary:
> According to Environment Canada (2009), many of our activities are dependent on water; therefore, protection of this natural resource is critical. Canadians are fortunate to have a wealth of fresh water, and we take advantage of this abundance by consuming more litres per day than residents in many other countries. Despite the luxury of plentiful water, we do have distribution challenges. Our water mostly runs north while our population is concentrated in the south.

MODEL 9 How to Write an Extended Persuasive Essay

Persuasive essays are written to persuade, or convince, people that a particular opinion about a topic is correct. The following guidelines will help you write an effective persuasive essay.

- Like all essays, a persuasive essay must have three general sections: an introduction, a body and a conclusion. In a short persuasive essay, the introduction and conclusion are usually one paragraph long, and the body of the essay has as many paragraphs as you have main points to make. However, in an extended persuasive essay, the introduction and conclusion may be more than one paragraph long, and the body of an extended essay has as many sections as you have main points to make. Each section may or may not be more than one paragraph long.

- The introduction announces the topic of the essay. Although there are many good ways to start an essay, the introduction usually begins with a general statement about why the topic is important.

- The introduction finishes with a *thesis statement*. A thesis statement is a sentence that includes the topic of the essay and the opinion that the essay will present. It may or may not include the main reasons why the opinion of the essay is correct.

- The body of the essay will contain a number of sections. For an extended persuasive essay, usually each section explains one reason why the essay opinion is correct. Each section may or may not be more than one paragraph long. The number of paragraphs per section depends on the content.

- Each section should start with a topic sentence that clearly indicates the topic of the section. You can do this by repeating key words (or a synonym of the key words) from the thesis.

- Within each section, each paragraph should start with a topic sentence that clearly indicates the topic of the paragraph and how it relates to the main point of the section.

- Each body paragraph should finish with a sentence that makes the point of the paragraph clear.

- The conclusion summarizes the main reasons why the essay opinion is correct. It often finishes with a sentence that restates (but not repeats) the thesis.

Example of an Extended Persuasive Essay

Water redistribution is the key to solving global water shortages. Agree or disagree and explain why.

WRITER'S PLAN	
INTRODUCTION	Water redistribution is no longer the key to solving global water shortages. There are other methods that will do a better job of eliminating water shortages.
REDISTRIBUTION	• historically: redistribution by dams and pipes • now: too many dams (give numbers) • no new rivers to dam • now what?
NOT USEFUL METHODS OF REDISTRIBUTION	• glaciers • water bags • old oil tanker

Are there really water shortages?
Some people don't agree with this statement. They say
• aquifers may be only temporarily low: in the process of establishing a steady state we can adapt to sinking ground levels;
• scientists will develop new technologies to eliminate the threat of water shortages.
However, this is a minority viewpoint.

What can be done about water shortages?	**OTHER METHODS**		
	• desalination • atmospheric water vapour processing • elimination of poverty • education and conservation		

DESALINATION	**WATER VAPOUR**	**POVERTY**	**EDUCATION**
• ocean water • energy consumption • waste product	• humid air • energy consumption • pure water	• complex • essential to address	• long-term • essential

CONCLUSION	• water redistribution is no longer the best method to solve water shortages • other methods, although they have drawbacks, are much more effective • desalination, water vapour processing, as well as the elimination of poverty and education and conservation will be more efficient in solving the world's water shortages

Meeting the Challenge of Water Shortages

Water shortages are fast becoming a fact of life, not only in undeveloped countries, but also in developed countries. Even those countries with the money to spend on wells, pumps, pipes and distribution systems are running out of water. The solution to this problem seems simple. If there is a shortage of water in one place and an abundance of water in another place, all that is required is the transportation of the water to the area without water. In fact, water shortages are complex problems; simple redistribution of water is no longer the most effective method of solving global water shortages.

Historically, redistribution of water has been very successful at eliminating water shortages. This redistribution was achieved by building dams on rivers, blocking the natural flow of water, and creating a reservoir, or extra water storage, above the dam. And while the dams have created environmental disruptions, they have been successful in sharing water amongst regions. However, today, the world's major rivers have all been dammed.[1] Any river left to be dammed is too small, or too distant. The cost of building dams on the remaining rivers is too high. As a result, the traditional method of redistributing water through a dam is no longer economically possible.

Other methods of redistribution have been proposed. Scientists have tried towing glaciers from the poles to warmer countries where water shortages exist; however, the glaciers melted too quickly.[2] A number of people have tried to float fresh water, contained in huge bags, through the ocean to thirsty countries. But the water bags remain theoretical.[3] Others have suggested water be carried in tanker ships that are too old to carry oil. But the costs of cleaning the tanker ships are too high.[4] There have always been theories about how water could be redistributed, but for reasons of cost and politics, these theories have not been achieved. With the limited number of rivers left to dam, and the high cost of other redistribution methods, this is no longer the most efficient way of preventing water shortages.

It is important to consider if there really are water shortages. There are some scientists that believe that although there may be water shortages, there is no crisis. These people point out that shrinking aquifers may simply be moving to a new steady state, and that we do not know enough about replenishment cycles of aquifers to know if they are really disappearing. These scientists suggest humans need only to adapt to sinking ground levels due to groundwater withdrawal; and they recommend people put their faith in emerging technologies to solve any water crisis in the future. However, this is a minority view. Most scientists point to prolonged water shortages in undeveloped countries, California, the shrinking of the Aral Sea in former Soviet Asia and the depleting of the aquifer under Mexico City as examples that a water crisis is not looming in the future, but here now, in the present. The vice-president of the World Bank, Ismail Serageldin states, "The wars of the next century will be about water."[5]

As the majority of scientists believe there really is a water crisis, other ways of addressing the problem of global water shortages must be considered. Desalination, or the process of removing salt from ocean water, is a reality in the Middle

---

1. Cameron, S.D. (1999, October/November). *Equinox, 107,* 33.
2. de Villiers, M. (1999). Solutions and manifestos. In *Water* (p. 332). Toronto, ON: Stoddart.
3. de Villiers, M. (1999). Solutions and manifestos. In *Water* (p. 328). Toronto, ON: Stoddart.
4. de Villiers, M. (1999). Solutions and manifestos. In *Water* (p. 332). Toronto, ON: Stoddart.
5. Cameron, S.D. (1999, October/November). *Equinox, 107,* 32.

East. This solution has the advantage of a water source that is easily available, provided a piece of coastline is accessible. Desalinated water from the ocean can then be pumped inland. This process consumes a lot of energy and produces some waste products, but these wastes can be properly managed so as not to damage the environment. Desalination is more than just a theory. It works in reality to fight water shortages.

Furthermore, atmospheric water vapour processing is providing hope for many areas experiencing water shortages. Water vapour processing pulls water vapour from warm, humid air, and cools and condenses it into pure water. Processors have been used in countries where there have been natural disasters in order to provide clean drinking water. For example, after an earthquake hit Taiwan in 1999, water vapour processors produced enough water to supply the military soldiers who were helping the relief efforts. The main source of water for this kind of treatment is humid air, which is free in large quantities. This technology is already fighting water shortages.

Len Abrams, in his paper entitled "Poverty and water supply and sanitation services,"[6] argues that poverty is at the root of all chronic water shortages. He states that governments that can't raise taxes to finance water supply systems can't build or maintain a water supply for their populations. Similarly, individuals who are poor do not have enough money to pay for basic services like water and education. Although this is not an easy solution, Abrams concludes that the best way to eliminate water shortages is to fight poverty.

Education about water conservation is also essential in the struggle against water shortages. In order to preserve water quantity and quality, people must learn how to conserve water around their homes and industries. Information about waste disposal and pollutants must become common knowledge, so water quality is protected. Again, this is a long-term solution, but still essential in order to eliminate water shortages.

It is clear now that water shortages are becoming a fact of life in all countries of the world. Traditional methods of water redistribution, building dams, are no longer possible, and other redistribution theories are too costly. Other methods, although they have drawbacks, are much more effective at addressing water shortages today. Desalination, water vapour processing, as well as the elimination of poverty and education and conservation will be methods scientists use to solve the global water shortages of tomorrow.

---

6. Abrams, L. (1999, November 29). Poverty and water supply and sanitation services. Retrieved from: http://www.thewaterpage.com

PHOTO CREDITS

CORBIS

Cover: © Ocean/Corbis

ISTOCKPHOTO

pp. ix (top), 114–115, 135: sjlocke
pp. ix (middle), 136–137, 155: travellinglight

SHUTTERSTOCK

pp. viii (top), 2–3, 23: Gabi Moisa
pp. viii (middle top), 24–25, 49: Diego Cervo
pp. viii (middle), 50–51, 69: sashagala
pp. viii (middle bottom), 70–71, 89: Patryk Kosmider
pp. viii (bottom), 90–91, 113: Yanik Chauvin
pp. ix (bottom), 156–157, 177: Goydenko Tatiana
p. 4: Petur Asgeirsson
p. 6: Christopher Halloran
p. 8: Bobby Johnson
p. 10: aceshot1
p. 11: Clive Watkins
p. 12 (left): Joe Belanger
p. 12 (right): fstockfoto
p. 13: Petur Asgeirsson
p. 15: ambrozinio
p. 17: Sergii Figurnyi
p. 19: Galina Barskaya
p. 20: Nagel Photography
p. 25 (right): William Perugini
p. 26: jokerpro
p. 27: Quang Ho
p. 28: Yuri Arcurs
p. 29 (left): corepics
p. 29 (right): Deymos
p. 30: Supri Suharjoto
p. 36: Raisman
p. 39: Iurii Davydov
p. 42: Yuri Arcurs
p. 44: Mike Flippo
p. 46: Zurijeta
p. 51: Losevsky Pavel
p. 52: Tyler Olson
p. 54: Elena Elisseeva
p. 55: ARENA Creative
p. 58: Alena Root
p. 59: iofoto
p. 60: F.CHI
p. 62: Blend Images
p. 63: Arthur Eugene Preston
p. 64: Rido
p. 66: Monkey Business Images
p. 73: Nagy-Bagoly Arpad
p. 74 (top right): Rafal Olechowski
p. 74 (bottom left): Daniel Gale

p. 76: yo-ichi
p. 78: filmfoto
p. 79: xtrekx
p. 80: Olaru Radian-Alexandru
p. 81: Robnroll
p. 82: Yuri Arcurs
p. 85: Baevskiy Dmitry
p. 86: zhu difeng
p. 87: Dmitriy Shironosov
p. 88: wrangler
p. 93 (left): Andre Blais
p. 93 (right): Poznyakov
p. 94: OLJ Studio
p. 95: fotohunter
p. 97: marilyn barbone
p. 98: Rainer Plendl
pp. 105, 107, 110: Yuri Arcurs
p. 112: wavebreakmedia ltd
p. 117: greenland
p. 118: Mike Tan C.T.
p. 119: jang14
p. 121: Bork
p. 122: bikeriderlondon
p. 126: Marlon Lopez
p. 127: Rob Marmion
p. 129: Sura Nualpradid
p. 131: H. Brauer
p. 133: Reda
p. 139: Copestello
p. 141: Gorilla
p. 142: Dmitrijs Dmitrijevs
p. 145: Zurijeta
p. 146: @erics
p. 148: RoxyFer
p. 150: James Peragine
p. 152: Kzenon
p. 160: Mona Makela
p. 161: Jiri Hera
p. 162: Gorilla
p. 164: FunStudio
p. 165: Dominik Michalek
p. 166: Lulu Durand
p. 167: WimL
p. 168: auremar
p. 171: B Brown
p. 173: Lincoln Rogers

NOTES

NOTES

NOTES

NOTES